THE
MARSHALL CAVENDISH
ILLUSTRATED ENCYCLOPEDIA
OF
DISCOVERY
AND
EXPLORATION

Spanish friars are slain by embittered Indians.

THE
MARSHALL CAVENDISH
ILLUSTRATED ENCYCLOPEDIA
OF
DISCOVERY
AND
EXPLORATION

VOLUME 4

GOD, GOLD AND GLORY
Nicholas Hordern

EDITORIAL COORDINATION
Beppie Harrison, John Mason
REVISION EDITOR
Donna Wood

Marshall Cavendish

New York · London · Toronto · Sydney

EDITORIAL STAFF
Executive Coordinators
Beppie Harrison
John Mason

Design Director
Guenther Radke

Editorial
Ann Craig
Maureen Matheson
Damian Grint
Lee Bennett
Marjorie Dickens
Jill Gormley
Isobel Campbell
Gail Roberts

Picture Editor
Peter Cook

Research
Ann Reading
Enid Moore
Sarah Waters
Margery MacLaren
Patricia Quick

Cartography
Geographical Projects

REVISION STAFF
Editor
Donna Wood

Editorial Director
Mark Dartford

Production Executives
Robert Paulley
John Collins

Editorial Contributors
Shane Winser
Robin Kerrod
Shane Roe

Art Editor
Janina Samoles

Picture Researcher
Moira McIlroy

Reference Edition Published 1990
© Marshall Cavendish Limited 1990
© J G Ferguson Publishing Company/Aldus Books Ltd. 1971

Published by Marshall Cavendish Corporation
147 West Merrick Road, Freeport, Long Island, NY 11520

Printed by Mladinska knjiga, jugoslavija
Bound in Italy by L.E.G.O. S.p.A., Vicenza

Library of Congress Cataloging-in-Publication Data
Discovery and exploration.
   Summary: Describes the journeys of the world's explorers from the
first men who traveled beyond the then-known world to the scientific
explorations of today.
   ISBN 1-85435-114-1
   1. Discoveries (in geography) – Juvenile literature.
[1. Discoveries (in geography)   2. Explorers.]
G175, D57 1990
910'. 9 – dc20   89-15723
                                                                      CIP
                                                                       AC

ISBN 1-85435-123-0   God, Gold and Glory

Introduction

The dramatic saga of Man's exploration of his world; his courage and endurance against all odds, is expertly told in the seventeen volumes of the *Discovery and Exploration* encyclopedia.

The exploits of the first intrepid adventurers from Phoenicia, Greece and Rome on their perilous journeys into the unknown, exploration in the Dark Ages which ventured west to the Atlantic and across Asia to China, and the charting of the vast Pacific, a huge area of bleak, unyielding ocean from which many ships did not return, shows the determination of these early explorers in their search for even greater knowledge of the world about them.

Covered in these volumes are the oldest trades routes toward the spice and treasure of the Orient and the merchants who discovered them, the ruthless Conquistadors who put their thirst for gold above all else and the pioneering trappers and traders who were responsible for opening up North America. The motives of many of these men may have been purely mercenary, but we still owe them the debt of their discoveries, the roots of which still exist in customs and practices in many parts of the modern world to this day.

Painstakingly researched and minute in detail, these volumes of *Discovery and Exploration* contain a record of almost every important geographical discovery to take place in the history of mankind. Highly illustrated with a wealth of ancient documents, contemporary paintings, maps and illuminating extracts from the explorers' personal accounts of their journeys, these books make fascinating reading and are visually exciting; quite different from the dry works of reference that many of us are used to.

These are real adventure stories, telling of the explorers who broke through the barriers of their time regardless of personal hardship.

The later volumes move on in time to the great discoveries of the 17th, 18th and 19th centuries: the colonization and exploration of Australia and New Zealand, the taming of the Sahara and the unique challenge represented by Africa and Asia, lands of savagery and suffering to the often ill-prepared explorers of bygone days.

Some relatively recent exploration work occupies the final volumes of the set; the journeys to the North and South Poles, undersea exploration by pioneers like Jacques Cousteau, the endeavors of some famous mountaineers and, lastly, a history of man's foray into space and his achievements there. An 80 page Index volume completes the set.

Contents

**VOLUME 4
GOD, GOLD & GLORY**

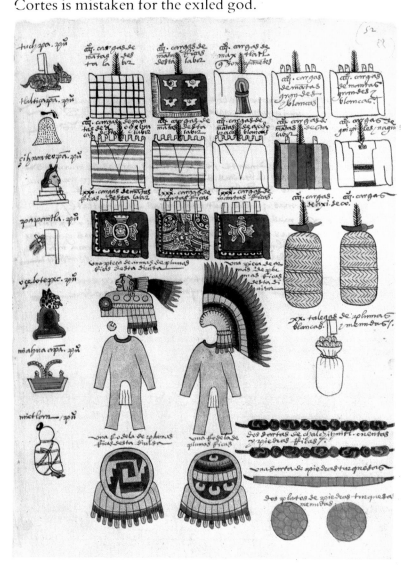

Aztec tribute list from the Codex Mendoza. The first column lists the Mexican towns that paid an annual tribute to the Aztec. The remaining illustrations show the types of tribute paid – among them cloth, warrior costumes, and cacao beans.

Spanish friar baptizes a Mexican Indian. Large numbers of priests accompanied the conquistadors to the New World in order to convert the Indians to Christianity.

The New World
1

"It was easy going at first. The thinner air of 8,000 feet refreshed me. New summits slid into view on the far horizon. I felt utterly alone .... Then I rounded a knoll and almost staggered at the sight I faced. Tier upon tier of Inca terraces rose like a giant flight of stairs.... Each terrace, hundreds of feet long, was banked with massive stone walls up to 10 feet high ... what group of Incas had needed a hundred such terraces in this lofty wilderness? ... Suddenly breathless with excitement, I forgot my fatigue and.... I plunged once more into damp undergrowth ... fought my way forward through vines and foliage.... A mossy wall loomed before me, half hidden in the trees. Huge stone blocks seemed glued together, but without mortar—the finest Inca construction.... It was part of a ruined house. Beyond it stood another, and beyond that I could make out more houses encased in twining growth...."

So exclaimed Hiram Bingham, a young American historian, when he accidentally stumbled on the stone city of Machu Picchu high in the Peruvian Andes. The year was 1911. Bingham had been searching for the ruins of the last known Inca stronghold. Now before him lay

Left: the Inca fortress-city of Machu Picchu, situated in an inaccessible corner of the Peruvian Andes. Machu Picchu, the last stronghold of the Inca Indians, was never found by the Spanish conquistadors. With its rows of terraces, its imposing temples, and its handsome palaces, the city remains virtually intact. It was discovered by Hiram Bingham in 1911.

Right: a Peruvian warrior as pictured on a pre-Inca pottery vase, of about A.D. 600–800. The Indian warrior is dressed for battle. He wears a helmet and carries a shield on his right arm.

not just another collection of ruins, but an entire terraced city of palaces, temples, towers, military barracks, connecting stairways, and fountains fed by aqueducts. In this inaccessible corner of the Andes, some 400 years earlier, the last remnant of the once mighty Inca army managed to defy the Spaniards for over 30 years. The city of Machu Picchu, hanging atop sheer precipices 1,000 feet high and girt by rapids that were impassable for six months of the year, must have been ideal for their purpose.

Hiram Bingham's spectacular discovery rekindled popular interest in the archaeology of the Americas, not only of the Inca in Peru, but also in all those places where silent, mysterious citadels of stone told of once flourishing civilizations. Who were the people who had hewn cities out of solid granite with only hammers and short crowbars for tools? How had they learned the skills to turn each project into an object of lasting beauty? And, above all, where had these ancient architects come from?

Most experts agree that the American Indians are descendants of men from Asia who crossed the Bering Strait to North America at least 20,000 years ago. The first human discoverer of America was probably an Asian nomad clad in animal skins and armed with a club and stone-pointed spear. He was a hunter, and, like most hunters, was forced to follow the migration of his prey—the mammoth, the mastodon, and the giant bison. Until the end of the last Ice Age around 10,000 years ago, it is probable that he, together with successive waves of hunters, crossed from Asia to North America over a bridge of land that spanned the Bering Strait.

In their endless search for game—and, we can guess, for warmer, more hospitable regions—the descendants of this primitive hunter pushed south. Over a period of hundreds, or perhaps thousands of years, they reached the picturesque Valley of Mexico, an elevated tableland between the two ranges of the Sierra Madre Mountains. Then they continued on to the lowlands of the Yucatán Peninsula in Latin America. Crossing the Isthmus of Panama to South America, they moved into the towering Andes, spread out over the Amazon Valley, and finally reached Tierra del Fuego, the southernmost tip of the Americas.

For thousands of years, man in the Americas lived the life of the nomad hunter. When he killed a mammoth, he gorged himself on its meat. When his crude weapons proved inadequate or when game was scarce, he went hungry. But man survived in the New World. His was a lasting conquest.

Then, beginning about 6,500 B.C.—in the highlands of Mexico—man in the Americas turned to agriculture. The cultivation of crops freed him from the uncertainties of the chase. It provided him with a permanent home within a rapidly expanding community and afforded him leisure to explore social, religious, and artistic pursuits. This development in the Americas was closely paralleled in the Old World where farming began in the fertile crescent of the Near East along the banks of the Euphrates and Tigris rivers. In

Above: façade of the building of *Las Manjas* (the nuns) at Chichén-Itzá. The building is elaborately ornamented with figures and hieroglyphs and is typical of Maya architecture of the Classical Period. This sketch was made by the Victorian architect and historian, Frederick Catherwood.
Left: the Olmec civilization flourished in Mexico until about A.D. 200. Some scholars believe Olmec ceramic figures, with their almond eyes, were influenced by early Asiatic visitors to the Americas.

both these regions, agriculture was introduced more than 7,000 years ago with wheat in the Old World and corn in the New. Some people see more than a coincidence between the two developments.

In the 1840's, when the American traveler John L. Stephens first glimpsed the stone ruins of the Maya civilization in the depths of the Honduran jungle, he felt compelled to comment: "savages never reared these structures." Stephens' opinion prevailed during the 1800's. Whenever vestiges of advanced civilizations were found in the Americas, they were attributed invariably to the direct influence of the Egyptians, Greeks, Phoenicians, Chinese, British, Irish, or

UNITED STATES

Colorado

SACRAMENTO MTS.

Río Bravo del Norte

Río Grande

-30°

110°

100°

90°

Yaqui

SIERRA MADRE OCCIDENTAL

SIERRA MADRE ORIENTAL

Fuerte

• Torreón

• Monterrey

G U L F   O F

TROPIC OF CANCER

MEXICO

M E X I C O

Rió Grande de Santiago

C. Corrientes

• León

-20°

Yucatan

C. Catoche

Guadalajara •

Mexico City

• Veracruz

POPOCATÉPETL
17,887   Puebla   • ORIZABA
18,701

Rió de las Balsas

SIERRA MADRE DEL SUR

Acapulco •

Isthmus
of
Tehuantepec

• Belize City

BELIZE

SA. MADRE

GUATEMALA   **HONDUR**

Guatemala •

Tegucigalpa •

San
Salvador •

EL SALVADOR

NICAR

Managua •

P A C I F I C   O C E A N

-10°

• 110°

0   100   200   300   400   500
Miles

100°

90°

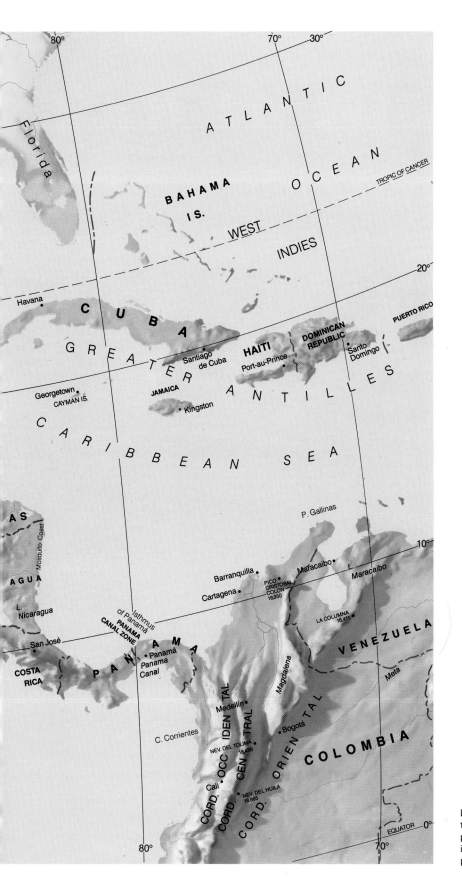

80°   70°   30°

ATLANTIC

Florida

BAHAMA
IS.

OCEAN   TROPIC OF CANCER

WEST

INDIES

20°

Havana

CUBA

PUERTO RICO

GREATER

Santiago
de Cuba   HAITI   DOMINICAN
REPUBLIC
Port-au-Prince   Santo
Domingo

Georgetown
CAYMAN IS.   JAMAICA

ANTILLES

Kingston

CARIBBEAN   SEA

P. Gallinas

AS
Mosquito Coast   10°

Barranquilla   Maracaibo   L.
PICO
CRISTOBAL   Maracaibo
COLON
AGUA   Cartagena   18,950

LA COLUMNA
16,411

Nicaragua
Isthmus
of Panama   VENEZUELA
PANAMA
CANAL ZONE   Panamá   Meta
San José   Panama
Canal

COSTA   PANAMA
RICA

C. Corrientes   Medellín   Magdalena   Bogotá

NEV. DEL TOLIMA
18,436   COLOMBIA

Cali   NEV. DEL HUILA
18,865

EQUATOR   0°

80°   70°

Left: Mexico, Central America, and
the Caribbean Sea, showing the
principal physical features, the
important cities, and the major
political frontiers.

13

Norsemen—never, it seems, to the American Indians themselves.

No doubt America did have some chance contact with the outside world before its discovery by Christopher Columbus in 1492. Evidence of such contact is found in the early hybridization of wild American cotton with the cultivated Asian variety. Additional proof is seen in the ancient ceramics found recently on the coast of Ecuador. These ceramics are similar in detail to pottery made in Japan between 3,000 and 2,000 B.C. The logical explanation is that they were carried by boat across the Pacific Ocean.

But the American continents are separated from the rest of the world by the world's two largest oceans. Moreover, the Old World civilization was in many ways quite distinct from that in the Americas. Eurasian civilization was based on the wheel, domesticated cattle, wheat and rice, the plow, the written alphabet, and the use of metals—bronze, iron, and steel—for tools. With the exception perhaps of bronze, which was invented without contact with the

Above: the pyramid and Temple of the Inscriptions at Palenque in southern Mexico. Palenque was built during the Classic Period of the ancient Maya civilization and represents the peak of Maya achievement in architecture and the arts. For hundreds of years after the decline of the Maya civilization, the city remained buried under dark, tangled rain forests. It was discovered by the Spaniards in 1748.

Right: a page from the Dresden codex, one of the three pre-conquest Maya codices that survived the zealous book burning of Spanish friars. The page contains elaborate astronomical calculations on the planet Venus.

Eastern Hemisphere, the New World was not acquainted with any of these. Quite independently, however, it cultivated food items that today comprise well over half the world's supply of agricultural products, such as corn, potatoes, chocolate, tomatoes, beans, squash, chili peppers, pumpkins, pineapples, avocadoes, papaya, and peanuts —all of which were unknown to the Old World.

It now seems entirely possible that the American pre-Columbian civilizations developed with only sporadic contact with Europe. And the people who created these separate civilizations did so with minimal contact among themselves. When the Europeans arrived in the Western Hemisphere, the three areas that had advanced the furthest were located in enclaves set physically apart from one another: the Maya in the lowland area of southern Mexico and Central America; the Aztec in the highland plateau of central Mexico; the Inca in the sealed desert and Andean kingdoms of South America.

The first Europeans in the New World encountered the most brilliant of all the pre-Columbian civilizations, that of the mysterious and enigmatic Maya. While Europe was in its "Dark Ages"—the period preceding the Renaissance—the Maya civilization was at its peak. From about A.D. 350 to the 800's, the Classic Period of the ancient Maya civilization, the Maya built over 100 city-states in the highlands of Guatemala and Honduras, southern Mexico, and the Yucatán Peninsula. These towns were hewn out of dense jungle with primitive tools and without the aid of wheels or beasts of burden. They were centers for religious and civil events, rather than cities for habitation. Most of the Maya were farmers who lived in outlying agricultural communities within reach of the towns.

The thriving production of corn enabled the Maya to turn to the pursuit of mathematics, astronomy, art, and religion. Religion was the driving force behind their great achievements. All effort was directed toward gaining the indulgence of the gods whose favor regulated the abundance or paucity of the crops. To appease their

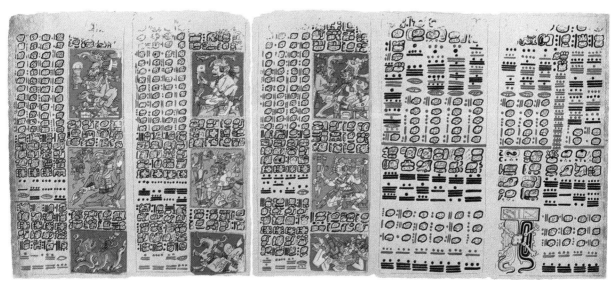

gods, the Maya offered animal and human sacrifices, and built magnificent temples, palaces, pyramids, and plazas in their honor. They studied astronomy so that planting and harvesting, sacrifices and other religious rituals, could be aligned with the day and hour most pleasing to the gods. They evolved a calendar based on these astronomical observations, as well as a system of numbers and a method of writing. Priests acted as intermediaries between the deities and the people, and were responsible for interpreting the gods' wishes. They provided for the future by teaching architecture, astronomy, astrology, chronology, writing, sculpture, and painting.

During the 700's, Maya architecture and art reached its peak. Then suddenly, and inexplicably, all collapsed. By A.D. 964, the disintegration of the Maya civilization was complete. What happened? Perhaps there was a series of disastrous earthquakes, a rampant epidemic, revolution, foreign invasion, or a severe change in climate. Until all the hieroglyphs engraved on Maya pillars and temples can be deciphered, the mystery will remain.

The chances of ever finding out were rendered slim because of a zealous Franciscan friar, Diego de Landa. In the 1500's, De Landa consigned the ancient Maya library to the flames because he thought the books "contained nothing but superstitions and falsehoods of the Devil." Of the thousands of books painted on bark-cloth paper

Right: "Arraignment of the Prisoners," a scene from the wall paintings at Bonampak, an ancient Maya ruin. On the upper tier stand richly attired priests and nobles. Below them, awaiting sentence, sprawl the prisoners of war. Various minor officials and attendants are ranged on the lower terrace. The Maya were skilled in the art of narrative painting. The bright colors and absence of perspective create a rich, decorative effect.

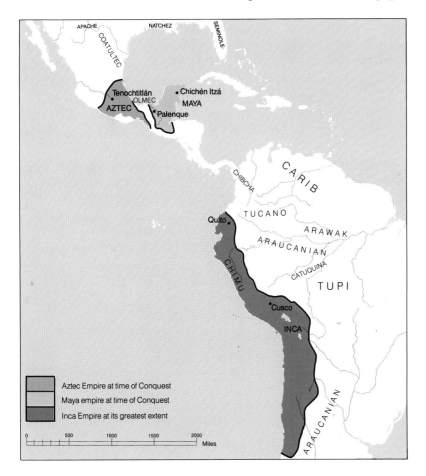

Aztec Empire at time of Conquest

Maya empire at time of Conquest

Inca Empire at its greatest extent

Left: Mexico, Central, and South America, showing the areas dominated by the Aztec, Maya, and Inca empires at the time the Spanish conquistadors arrived and began steadily to overcome and crush them. The map also shows many of the other Indian tribes with whom the explorers came in contact.

(*codices*) only three fragmented specimens survive. The entire recorded history of a unique civilization was reduced to ashes.

The second period, known as the Mexican Period (about A.D. 900–1519), originated on the northern plains of Yucatán where the Toltec Indians formed a kingdom with its capital located at Chichén Itzá. The result was a vigorous renaissance of the Maya civilization. Architecture took on new dimensions of space and elegance that surpassed even that of the Classic Period. But in other respects the new empire fell short of its predecessor. Though more lavish, it introduced little that was really new. After 450 years of political cohesion, the kingdom dissolved. Civil wars dominated the life of the region. The first European visitors were to see the Maya civilization in its final stages of decay.

Left: turquoise mosaic knife carved in the shape of a crouched warrior. It was used at the sacrificial altar. Below: the Aztec practiced various forms of human sacrifice, the most common being the removal of the heart from a living victim. The man to be sacrificed was held by attendants while a priest tore open his chest and plucked out the still-beating heart. An early Spanish chronicler records that the number of men sacrificed in a single year exceeded 50,000.

The Aztec Empire

2

In the late 1300's, a barbarian tribe from the north of Mexico moved south and entered the beautiful Valley of Mexico. They were the Aztec. Wherever the unwelcome intruders tried to settle, they were swiftly ejected by the already civilized Indian inhabitants. In about 1325, after years of struggle, the Aztec established their capital, Tenochtitlán, now Mexico City, on a forlorn little island in Lake Texcoco. Tradition states that here the tribal elders had seen the sign that their god, Huitzilopochtli, had told them to look for—an eagle (symbol of the sun and Huitzilopochtli) perched on a cactus and eating a serpent. That sign of the Aztec priests remains the Mexican emblem to this day. One hundred and fifty years later, the Aztec had conquered vast territories stretching from the coast of the Gulf of Mexico to the Pacific and as far south as Guatemala.

The meteoric rise of the Aztec can be more easily understood when it is seen as the culmination of a remarkable cultural sequence that began in the pre-Christian era and was continued by the archaic cultures of the Maya and the Toltec. What others had created, the Aztec adapted and refined. They were the inheritors, rather than the originators of their civilization. But, like the Romans, they were responsible for preserving and spreading that culture throughout the lands they conquered.

In certain aspects the Aztec culture never reached the excellence of the Maya. Their writing was closer to elementary pictorial representation than to the more advanced hieroglyphic form. But like the Maya and other Mexican civilizations, the Aztec had a strong historic sense and fine tradition of picture writing. Painted books recorded their history, laws, rites, and ceremonies. The books were pictorial and were essentially only lists of events that served as memory aids to Aztec historians. Most pre-conquest manuscripts were systematically destroyed by the Spaniards, but the tradition continued during the colonial period and many early Spanish chroniclers based their writings on earlier Mexican manuscripts.

In art, craftsmanship, agriculture, and architecture, the Aztec excelled in their own right. From European eyewitnesses, we hear of the sheer splendor of the temples and palaces, the flourishing state of the agriculture, and the exquisite nature of the works of art executed by highly skilled Aztec craftsmen.

The warlike Aztec established an empire that was constantly expanding. In less than 200 years, the once barbarian Aztec had

Above: the *Mapa de Santa Cruz*, an early plan of Mexico City and Lake Texcoco, shows the network of canals and causeways linking the city with the surrounding mainland. The Aztec artist has decorated the map with scenes of everyday Indian life. The lake is filled with boats and fishermen; the roads are crowded with Indian porters, hunters, and travelers.

Left: turquoise mosaic mask of the Aztec god Quetzalcoatl. The mask was placed over the effigy of the god at certain religious festivals and upon the death of a king. It was sometimes placed upon the dead after they had been dressed for burial. The exquisite workmanship of this mask is a fitting tribute to Quetzalcoatl, god of learning.

developed a civilization that caused the leader of the Spanish conquistadors to declare their capital Tenochtitlán: "The most beautiful city in the world."

By 1500, Tenochtitlán had developed into a giant stone metropolis with a population of about 150,000. Three wide causeways joined the island to the mainland, and stone aqueducts carried drinking water from the springs of Chapultepec three miles away. The city was brilliantly colorful. Noblemen's villas, administration buildings, and temples were painted either a dazzling white or dull red. The houses had cool inner courtyards or patios containing fountains at the center. Inside, curtains and tapestries hung from ceilings inlaid with cedar and other exotic woods. The Spaniards called the Aztec capital "The Venice of the New World." They had good reason. This glittering city, lying on a turquoise lake more than 7,000 feet above sea level and overlooked by snow-capped volcanoes, was a sight matched only by Venice itself.

The 5-square-mile city had been enlarged by the invention of "floating gardens," the *chinampas*, and by the driving of piles into the lake bed. Chinampas were rafts constructed of silt and masses of rushes and reeds which, in the course of time, took root in the soil

Above: skilled craftsmen displayed and sold their wares, such as this exquisite turquoise mosaic, in the great market at Tenochtitlán. Made in the shape of a double-headed serpent, this pendant was probably meant for the adornment of an Aztec noble.

of the shallow lake bottom, and became islands. Some were 300 feet in length, long enough to allow the cultivation of fruits, vegetables, and the flowers particularly loved by the warlike Aztec. Although most of the lake has since dried up, chinampas can still be seen today southeast of Mexico City at Lake Xochimilco.

Although they had neither wheel nor beast of burden, the Aztec found transportation no problem. The streets of Tenochtitlán were canals over which boats could glide. Through the maze of canals, produce-laden canoes headed for Tlatelolco, the great market square in the northern section of the city. The Spaniards told of the "plaza ... where more than 60,000 souls gather daily, buying and selling ... and where merchants from 60 cities would display, jewelry of silver and gold, and precious stones, skins of deer, jaguar, and puma, pottery, and textiles, beautiful mosaics made from birds' feathers, honey, fish, venison, turkey, fattened hairless dogs, dyes for fabrics, tobacco, rubber, and much else besides."

In 1502, at the age of 35, Montezuma II ascended the throne of the Aztec empire. Most of Mexico's 11 million Indian inhabitants now owed allegiance to the new young ruler. In reality his empire was no more than a loose federation of city-states linked through a common fear of an overlord who demanded tribute, but offered little in the way of protection or benefits of any kind. Some cities of

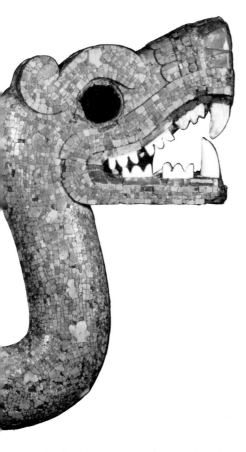

ancient Mexico, such as Tlaxcala and Tarascan, were never con-quered by the Aztec. But other, less powerful cities that disputed the demands of the Aztec were raided—their men and women hauled off to the capital for slavery, or worse, for human sacrifice. The god Huitzilopochtli was ever hungry for blood. In 1487, no less than 80,000 captured warriors and members of subject states were sacrificed to celebrate the opening of a great temple.

Under Montezuma's rule, political power was held by a ruling class based on birth but open to talent. At the top of the social pyramid stood Montezuma, who held religious and political authority as a priest and supreme chief. Contrary to the Spaniards' belief, he was not a hereditary ruler but an elected official who could be deposed if the high council grew dissatisfied with his performance. Of royal descent, Montezuma was well known before his election, both as a general in the army and as a priest. So powerful was the priesthood in Aztec life that it was the latter of the two offices

Right: Montezuma on the occasion of his election. The emperor is dressed in the traditional manner of the Aztec nobility, with a richly decorated cape and elaborate arm and leg orna-ments. The green quetzal feathers strapped to his back were the symbol or royalty and were identified with Quetzalcoatl, Aztec god of learning and of the priesthood.

Above: page from the Codex Zouche Nuttal, a Mixtec manuscript recounting the legend of an ancient Indian chief. Painted on a long strip of deerskin many years before the arrival of the Spaniards, the Codex Nuttal has been identified as one of the two books sent by Cortes to the Spanish king. It is perhaps the finest example of a pre-conquest Mexican painted book.

that proved more influential in his selection as emperor. In the chronicles of his Aztec contemporaries, Montezuma is described as "learned, an astrologer, a philosopher, and skilled in the arts."

Next in importance after the priests and nobles were the bureaucrats who handled the administrative chores of the state, and the merchants who traveled to all corners of the empire in pursuit of trade. Commerce was highly developed in the Aztec society. Often these merchants would combine diplomatic tasks with their own commercial ventures. They also provided information on new cities that could lead to an invasion of the territory. The artisans (sculptors, jewelers, weavers, masons) were next in rank. These were followed by the commoners and the peasants who tilled the land. The slaves—men captured in battle, or people sold into bondage for debt or other reasons—made up the lowest ranks of the Aztec social order. They were generally treated like the modern servant and their fate was quite different from the brutal and degrading

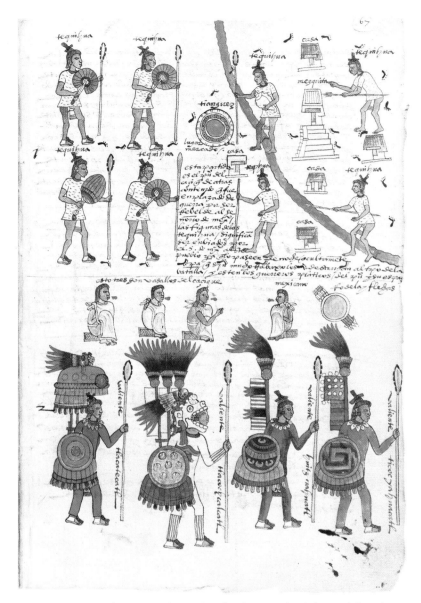

Left: an Aztec scouting expedition and punitive raid from the Codex Mendoza. This book was painted by an Indian artist after the Spanish conquest. Although it retains many of the characteristics of earlier Aztec manuscripts, it is a true "book" composed of folios and painted on European paper. The artist reflects the impact of European ideas in his use of perspective, line, and shading. (Bodleian Library, Oxford, MS. Arch. Selden A. 1. folio 67.)

treatment meted out to slaves in the later colonial era. The Aztec slave could marry at will and his offspring automatically assumed the full rights of a free citizen at birth.

Through all ranks of Aztec society, family and community were prized above all else, and a strong moral code prevailed. A surprisingly tender streak could always be detected beneath the warlike façade. A father counseled his son to: "Revere and greet your elders; console the poor and the afflicted with good works and words. . . . Follow not the madmen who honor neither father nor mother; for they are like animals, for they neither take nor hear advice. . . . Do not mock the old, the sick, the maimed, or one who has sinned. Do not insult or abhor them, but abase yourself before God and fear lest the same befall you. . . . Do not set a bad example, or speak indiscreetly, or interrupt the speech of another. If someone does not speak well or coherently, see that you do not do the same; if it is not your business to speak, be silent."

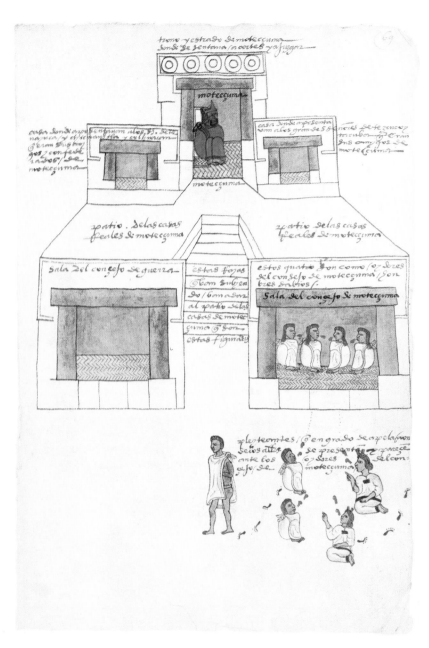

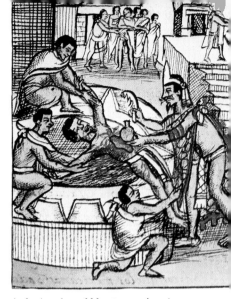

Left: drawing of Montezuma's palace depicts the emperor elevated and alone in his council chamber. Four judges sit in the Aztec court of appeal. Below them are the litigants (Bodleian Library, Oxford, MS. Arch. Selden A. 1. fol. 69.)

Despite its domestic tranquility, the Aztec state was constantly at war. Disturbances and uprisings punctuated the first 16 years of Montezuma's reign as one province after another sought to break away from the Aztec's harsh rule and warfare prevailed with neighboring powers. Montezuma was very much involved with affairs of state. However, he was also able to devote considerable time to religious matters and assumed an air of semi-divinity, which even extended to his dining habits. Thirty or more different dishes would be set before him, including turkey, quail, venison, pigeon, and hare. A favorite food was fresh fish, caught on the Gulf coast 200 miles away and brought by special couriers over the mountain passes. Beautiful, young handmaidens brought vessels containing water to

Above: Montezuma I (1390?–1469) attending a sacrifice in Tenochtitlán. Below: Aztec warriors wage a "flowery war" with their neighbors. The object of this ceremonial warfare was the capture of warriors for use as sacrificial victims.

bathe the emperor's hands between courses, and carefully placed a wooden screen before him so that he would be concealed from view while eating or while drinking from his golden goblets.

Cervantes de Salazar, a Spaniard, commented: "Toward his own people, Montezuma maintained a lofty majesty. With the exception of a few great lords of royal blood, Montezuma allowed no one to gaze upon his face, or to wear shoes, or sit down in his presence. He seldom left his chamber other than to eat, received few visitors, and conducted the bulk of his business through the members of his council. Even they contacted him through intermediaries. For the sacrifices at the temple of Huitzilopochtli, where he displayed great devotion, he made his way through his own quarters, remaining at some distance from the hierarchy, and returning downcast, deep in thought, speaking to no one."

Religion was the staff of life to the Aztec. The world seemed full of hostile natural forces whose power could be terrible if not assuaged. Drought, famine, thunderstorm, and earthquake were all occurrences fresh in the mind. The 40 or more deities in the Aztec pantheon were supposed to take care that these things did not

occur again. But the gods were hard to please. What they needed and wanted was the most valuable thing man could offer—life. The worse the predicament the more the gods needed propitiating. The sun was born every morning, and died at night. He battled with the elements of darkness before sunrise. If the battle was not won, it meant the destruction not only of Tenochtitlán but of the whole world. If the sun did not rise, nothing would live. The strength necessary for the sun god's victory was best supplied by an offering of human hearts, for that beating, blood-driving muscle was obviously the seat of life itself. As the chosen people of Huitzilopochtli the holy mission of the Aztec was to fight battles to capture prisoners whose hearts would be offered to appease the god's desire for blood. This sacred mission went hand in hand with the profane political drive to expand territory. Under the Aztec, then, there could be no peace. With peace there were no captured warriors, and with no captured warriors, the sun would go hungry. Even "flowery wars" were resorted to. These were "friendly" battles between states, with equal numbers on each side. The fighting ceased when both had enough captives to satisfy the appetites of their respective gods. The sun god, Huitzilopochtli, was insatiable.

But the Aztec also venerated another god, Quetzalcoatl, the god with a white face and a dark beard. As god of learning and the priesthood, Quetzalcoatl abhorred human sacrifice. It was he who instructed man in agriculture, the arts, and industry. Huitzilopochtli and Quetzalcoatl were forever locked in a titanic power struggle for supremacy of the universe. Through deceit and trickery on the

Below: the title page of the Codex Mendoza depicts an eagle, symbol of the sun and of Huitzilopochtli, perched on a cactus. According to ancient legend, Huitzilopochtli led his people to the shore of Lake Texcoco where, on seeing this omen, they founded the city of Tenochtitlán. God of the sun and warfare, Huitzilopochtli was the principal deity of the Aztec Indians. (Bodleian Library, Oxford, MS. Arch. Selden A. 1. folio 1.)

part of his rival, Quetzalcoatl had been driven away. He went east across the sea vowing that he would return in the year *Ce Acatl* (one reed), to avenge his downfall.

Ce Acatl years fell in 1363, 1467, and 1519. The year was now 1518. During the preceding years, the superstitious Montezuma had been disturbed by a series of portents that his priests, soothsayers, magicians, and other prophets were at a loss to interpret: the temple of Huitzilopochtli suddenly ablaze; a vertical sheet of flame in the east at midnight every night for a year; enormous comets blazing fiery trails across the skies in broad daylight; the lake flooding its banks as if in some tempestuous storm when not a breath of air could be felt; a woman wailing each night, ceaselessly, an eerie and sinister lament.

Then one day, a breathless messenger rushed up to the emperor and reported that he had seen "towers or small mountains floating on the waves of the sea" off the Gulf Coast. A second report said that the vessels bore strange people who "have very light skin, much lighter than ours. They all have long beards, and their hair comes only to their ears." No sooner had Montezuma's messengers exchanged greetings with the strangers from the east than the latter seemed ready to depart Aztec territory, promising to return the next year. This would be 1519, the year of Ce Acatl. The riddle of the omens was solved. The only thing left for an apprehensive Montezuma to do was to sit back and let the omniscient power struggle unfold before his eyes. Quetzalcoatl, true to his word, was coming back.

Below left: an Aztec priest observes the fiery trail of a comet from his rooftop. To the Aztec people, comets signified imminent death and destruction. A year before the Spaniards' arrival in Mexico, a series of comets was sighted. When reported to Montezuma, they were interpreted as heralding the end of the Aztec empire.

Below: Quetzalcoatl, the "Plumed Serpent," was a former culture hero of the Toltecs who was absorbed into the Aztec pantheon as god of learning and the priesthood. He instructed men in farming and the arts. Quetzalcoatl had been driven out of Mexico by Huitzilopochtli, but had promised to return and claim his lost empire. Montezuma believed Cortes to be the returned god.

Right: Manco Capac, the first Inca
ruler, as pictured by the Inca
artist, Poma de Ayala. Manco Capac
is said to have led the Inca people
to the Valley of Cuzco where he founded
the Inca empire around the year 1200.

Below: the towering snow-capped
peaks of the Andes Mountains stretch
along the entire west coast of South
America. They were the home of the
Inca Indians, one of the greatest of
pre-Columbian American civilizations.

The Land of the Inca

3

Far to the south of Mexico, centered in the Andes Mountains—the sturdy backbone of South America—the Inca empire stretched more than 2,500 miles from the Colombia-Ecuador border to central Chile. The Inca, like the Aztec, were latecomers. When they began their path of conquest that was to include parts of present-day Peru, northwestern Argentina, Bolivia, Chile, and Ecuador, they encountered civilizations that had been flourishing for hundreds of years. In the tremendous extremes of cold and heat, jungle, desert, and precipitous slope, the Inca came upon dwelling places which, through the resourcefulness and ingenuity of the inhabitants, had been made eminently habitable. Sophisticated networks of irrigation brought water to desolate wasteland. Agricultural terracing made farming possible on steep inclines. Aqueducts carried precious drinking water over distances of miles. Edible guinea pigs called viscacha were raised in many regions of the Andes. Herds of llamas, distant relatives of the camel, grazed on the mountain slopes where the cultivation of maize was impossible. Roads swept to remote corners of the Andes, formerly inaccessible to man or beast. Nature rewarded this industry with a bountiful return of food, sunshine, and clear blue skies. It also provided awesome natural barriers. However, these did have an advantage: they prevented the constant outbreaks of internecine warfare that had so often plagued the Mexican kingdoms to the far north.

The ancestors of the Inca Indians may have lived in Peru as early as 2,000 B.C. Until about A.D. 400, they were probably llama herders and potato growers in the high, inhospitable plains of the southern Peruvian highlands. As such they were indistinguishable from a host of other tribes in the vicinity. A popular Inca legend, however, gives a more colorful picture of their origin. The legend tells of four brothers and four sisters—the children of the Sun God—who emerged from a cave 18 miles southeast of Cuzco. People from adjoining caves accompanied them. These were the Inca. Led by Manco Capac, one of the four brothers, the group set out in search of better lands. They were armed with a golden divining rod which, when plunged into the fertile earth would sink deep into the ground indicating the spot where a new city should be built. Their journey was a leisurely affair during the course of which the leader's three brothers were conveniently disposed of in one way or another. This left the only remaining son of the Sun God as the first Inca ruler.

CVS

CO.

CVSCO. REGNI PERV IN NOVO ORBE CAPVT.

32

To maintain the purity of his divine descent, he married his elder sister, Mama Occlo. This incestuous marriage established a precedent that was to continue throughout the Inca dynasty. The Inca emperor, like the Inca nobles, was polygamous. However, his *coya* (official wife) was generally a sister, and the successor to the throne had to be a male issue from this union.

The small band descended into the attractive Valley of Cuzco, 11,440 feet above sea level. Because it is in the latitude of the tropics, the valley enjoys a delightful climate despite its high altitude. Here the soil is fertile, and the wooded, green meadows are watered by the Huatanay River. In this delightful spot, not surprisingly, the golden rod was put to work. According to one version of the legend, it sank so far down that it disappeared from view altogether. Thus, around A.D. 1200, the Inca capital, Cuzco, was born. But the fertile Valley of Cuzco was already occupied and the reception extended to the Inca was no less hostile than the one accorded to the nomadic, homeless Aztec who had entered the civilized Valley of Mexico much farther north at about the same time. They were unwelcome intruders. For the next 200 years the energies of the Inca were spent in warring with their neighbors.

In 1438, Pachacuti (over-turner of the earth) became the ninth emperor in the Inca dynasty. In the course of the next 55 years Pachacuti (1438–1471) and his son, Tupac Inca (1471–1493), conquered all of Peru and portions of Ecuador, Bolivia, and Chile. Pachacuti was more than just a conqueror. During his reign he founded a vast empire based on systematic lines. New cities that had been subdued by his armies were organized on Inca patterns, and administered by a hierarchy of officials directly responsible to the capital at Cuzco. All positions of consequence were held by the Inca, and posts—such as governorship of a region—were reserved for those of Inca royal blood. In little over 50 years, at least 12 million people had been welded together by the strength of Pachacuti and Tupac Inca. The Inca empire was made up of about 500 tribes, from very different geographic areas and often with separate customs, languages, occupations, and religions.

Cuzco had acquired a population in excess of 100,000 people, and had become the focal point of the Inca empire. The main feature of the city was the central plaza, from which the narrow streets flowed. The plaza was encircled by the emperor's palace, the prominent buildings of the nobility, and the temple complex. The walls of many prominent buildings were adorned with gold plate. Thatched roofs in the adjoining areas were interlaced with straws of gold that caught the first rays of the morning sun as it rose from behind the rim of the surrounding mountains.

The gold-plated Temple of the Sun dominated the square of the city, underlining its central importance as the religious hub of the empire. Pachacuti was not only head of state but, as the Inca emperor in direct descent from the Sun God, was regarded by the people as a living god. His every whim became instant law. Even the highest nobles entered his presence only after showing marks of deep humility, with the head bowed and the symbolic laborer's "pack" on the back.

There is a saying that while the Maya dreamed and the Aztec worshiped, the Inca built. The Maya and the Aztec reached a higher intellectual level. The Inca, on the other hand, preferred to build houses, palaces, cities, roads, bridges, irrigation projects, and agri-

Below: modern travelers follow an ancient Indian highway in Peru. Inca roads were marvels of engineering skills. They crossed mountains and deserts, bringing remote corners of the empire within traveling distance.

Above: drawing by an Indian artist showing Inca builders placing stones in the construction of a wall. This illustration, and others in the same sequence used in this book, are taken from Felipe Guaman Poma de Ayala's *Nueva coronica y buen gobieino*, dated about 1600, and now in the Royal Library, Copenhagen.

cultural terracing—all items of earthly endeavor. Although religion was part of their daily life, it did not control it. And as for sacrificing thousands of human lives to propitiate the gods, when they could be regularly employed on any number of construction projects, this seemed not only impractical, but also totally self-defeating.

The Inca were undoubtedly the master builders of the New World. A feature of their buildings was a massive simplicity endowed with beautiful proportions. Their only external ornamentation was the occasional gold and silver plate, or feathered mosaic mural decorations. Their architects designed buildings in which walls often sloped inward from the perpendicular. The plain surfaces were

Above: the baths at Tambo Machay, Peru, testify to the Inca's skill in stone masonry. The baths are constructed of various-sized granite blocks, fitted together without cement. They are placed so exactly that it is impossible to insert the point of a knife between them.

CONZEJO ALCALDE DE CORTE **HAMAUCVSCOYNGA** CAMACAPO·VATAC

ALGVAZIL MAIOR **CHACNAIKAMAIOC** LVRITACVSCO

COREGIDOR DE PROVINCIAS **TOCRICOCIVESMICHOC**

ADMINIITRADOR DE PROVINCIAS **SVIVIOCGVAIACPOMA**

| The palace mayor in Hanan Cuzco | The chief alguazil (constable) | The provincial corregidor (governor) | The provincial administrator |

GOVERNADOR DE LOS CAMINOS REALES **CAPACNIAN·TOCRICOC·AUTA** INGA

GOVERNADOR DE LOS PVENTES DE STER **CHACAS VIDIOC AGOSINGA** GUAMBOCHACA

SECRETARIO DEL INGA COZEJO **INCAROMPOCNINCADA** APOCONARCAMACHICVTININVIPOC

VECITADORI REVEDOR DE STOS REIÑOS **TARIPACOC·EDA PROVIGA**

| The inspector of the roads | The inspector of the bridges | The secretary of the Inca | The traveling inspector of the empire |

Above: the Inca evolved an elaborate and sophisticated bureaucratic system that enabled the vast empire to function smoothly. Hundreds of minor officials were appointed to take care of the everyday business of government.

broken up by slightly trapezoidal openings and niches that narrowed at the top. The close fitting of the gigantic boulders gave off a contrasting light and shadow effect, achieved from the hairline joints and the special texture of the rock itself. The result was not only decorative in effect but practical. The interlocking, mortarless pieces were capable of withstanding unusual stress and strain. The structures were impervious even to earthquakes that would shatter more recent and conventional masonry.

Pachacuti entrusted the active campaigning to his son, Tupac Inca, and resolved to spend his last years in overseeing Inca construction. The versatile Pachacuti displayed as much foresight in his architectural feats as in his empire building. He was responsible for laying-out Cuzco's streets on a grid system. He also contributed to the construction of what are considered the three most enduring monuments to Inca achievement in stone building: the Temple of the Sun at Cuzco, the Sacsahuaman fortress, and Machu Picchu, the city-fortress high above the Urabamba River Valley.

The Sacsahuaman fortress, high up on a hill behind Cuzco, was large enough to house the entire city. Hiram Bingham referred to

The royal courier

The Tahuantinsuyu supreme council

its northern wall as being "perhaps the most extraordinary structure built by ancient man in the Western Hemisphere."

In the aftermath of Cuzco's devastating earthquake in 1950, the colonial superstructure of the Monastery of Santo Domingo collapsed into a pile of bricks, cement, and other rubble. Its foundations, however, consisting of ground granite blocks prescribing a graceful arc, remained as secure as the day Pachacuti saw them being laid.

While Pachacuti built, his son and successor to the throne, Tupac Inca, increased the limits of the Inca empire. Advancing northwest from Cuzco, Tupac defeated the powerful kingdom of the Chimu. Only one kingdom of consequence was now left to conquer—Quito in what is now Ecuador. Tupac sent an ultimatum to Quito demanding immediate surrender. This was refused and a great battle lasting many months began. Eventually Tupac was victorious, thus gaining a province of great significance to the future of the empire.

The pattern of conquest began to acquire identifiable characteristics. First there was the diplomatic approach when prospective territories would be advised of the benefits of joining the Inca empire. If rhetoric or the sight of 70,000 lithe warriors on the

Above: a Mochica stirrup vase representing a Peruvian warrior. The Mochica-Chimu peoples possessed a great civilization, which rivaled that of the Incas. Their warriors were finally defeated by Tupac Inca in 1461.

Above: the most famous of the Inca bridges, spanning the precipitous gorge of the Apurimac River. The cables of plaited and twisted rope, as thick as a man's body, were over 250 feet long. Built in 1350, the Inca bridge continued in use until 1890.

skyline were not persuasive, then hostilities commenced. Generally, the opposing forces were overwhelmed, and an Inca garrison stationed in the newly won territory. Teams of engineers and administrators followed quickly in the wake of victory. The learning of the Quechuan language, the official language of the Inca and their provinces, was made compulsory. If the conquered people were acquiescent, they were free to retain their own rulers and system of government, but with an Inca advisor regulating policies. If troublesome, the whole populace was liable for mass deportation to a safer territory, and "friendly" citizens took their place in the new outpost of the empire.

Vital to the success of Inca military operations was the rapid communications system based on its vast network of roads. As the empire grew in size, it became doubly important to be in a position to deploy large forces with utmost speed. Ten thousand miles of paved roads crossed desert, jungle, and 15,000 foot Andean highlands alike. The largest of these was the Andean royal road that stretched 3,250 miles south down the mountain chain. The coastal desert road paralleled the highland, extending 2,520 miles to the south. Numerous lateral roads linked the two major highways. Bridges suspended by cable, or floating on pontoons (flat-bottomed boats), were flung across marshes, chasms, or other obstacles in the path of the long, straight roads. The most famous of these bridges spanned a 250-foot-wide gap between the precipices of the Apurimac River. Hung on rope suspension cables as thick as a man's body, the bridge was in use from the time the Inca built it around 1350 until 1890.

On the main highways, *tambos* (rest stations), were distanced 12 or 18 miles apart, depending on the terrain. These tambos acted as an invaluable logistical aid to armies on the move. They contained abundant stores of arms and food—mostly dried llama meat and dehydrated potatoes. Couriers were stationed about three miles apart to provide a messenger service unmatched for speed. Including all types of terrain, these couriers averaged an incredible speed of a mile in just over six minutes. The world record for this distance today is well under four minutes. Running in relays, Inca couriers could cover 150 miles in a day!

Oral messages were often supplemented by a device known as the *quipu*, the closest the Inca ever came to writing. The quipu consisted

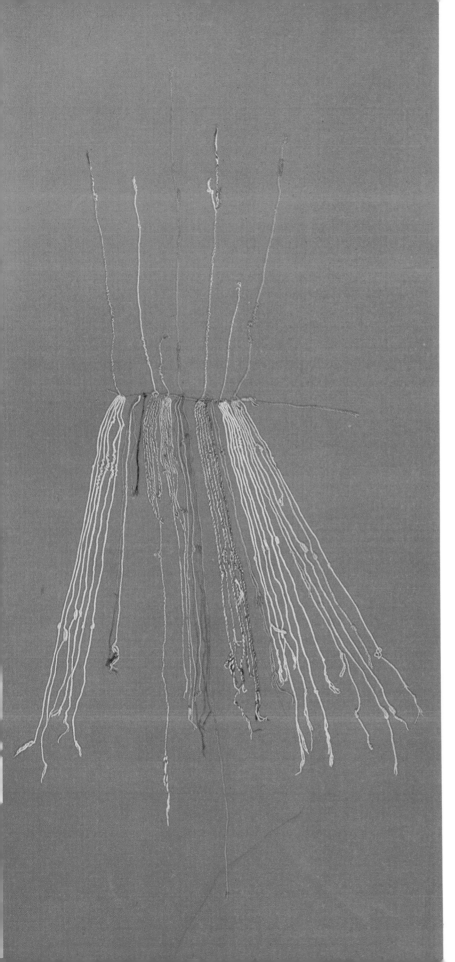

Above: an Inca official holding a quipu. A rapid communication system was vital to the vast Inca empire. Running in relays, messengers could cover about 240 miles a day, even over the most difficult terrain.

Left: the quipu was a device used by the Inca to keep accounts and to aid the memory in recording history and relaying messages. The quipu consisted of a main cord from which was hung many smaller strings, sometimes of different colors. Groups of knots, tied at intervals, indicated the number of a given item.

of one main strand of rope from which many smaller strings, sometimes of different colors, were hung. The position of the knots tied in the string would indicate the number of any given item, based on a decimal system. The strings indicated different objects, and even the way the thread was twisted or how the knot was tied, bore its special significance. Some claimed that it was even capable of conveying abstract ideas. Official court-appointed quipu readers (the best requiring a lifetime's familiarity with the technique) could catalog an entire inventory of a province down to the last head of llama or measure of maize. These keepers of the records would apply the quipu in their recitation of Inca history, an official version that camouflaged the existence of prior cultures in Peru.

In 1492, when Huayna Capac succeeded his father, Tupac Inca, on the throne, he presided over a vast domain that was at heart an agricultural society. At the lowest rung, the bulk of the population were the farmers. Their life was organized from the cradle to the grave by a bevy of supervisors at the family, village, tribal, provincial, regional, and national level. The Peruvian was the most resourceful and scientific farmer known to the ancient world. He made extensive use of such devices as highland terracing, irrigation, and fertilization to ensure a productive soil even in the most inaccessible of regions. In the highlands he herded cattle, such as the llama and alpaca. And, where his maize and other staple crops could not be grown due to the high altitude, he developed and gave to the world the white potato, quinoa (a cereal grain), and other plants. Plants with medicinal properties—such as quinine and cocaine—that are used still in modern medicine, originated first in Peru.

Land belonged to the state but was loaned out to the people according to their needs. Each citizen was obliged to provide one-third of his produce to the state and another third to the temple The remainder could be used for his own consumption. The very young, the old, and the infirm were provided with food and other articles free of charge. As private property was non-existent, theft was a crime against the state and was punishable by death. But if, for example, the food was stolen to prevent starvation, then the person prosecuted was not the thief but his overseer, for failing in his duty to provide the basic amenities for living. The submergence of the individual for the benefit of the community as a whole was ingrained in the discipline of Peruvian life. The gulf between the privileged

Above: this early Indian drawing shows a farmer irrigating land in ancient Peru. Inca methods of agriculture were the most advanced of any pre-Columbian civilization. Below: modern farmers near Cajamarca, Peru still use the methods of irrigation developed by the Inca Indians.

Left: this Peruvian agricultural deity, wearing a moon headdress, dates from between A.D. 600–1000. The body of the deity is decorated with maize and squash, the traditional foods of pre-Columbian America. The majority of the Inca were farmers and worshiped gods of the land.

and the common folk was very great, but none went hungry and military protection was guaranteed to all.

In 1524, the Inca encountered their first white man when the Chiriguano Indians attacked a southern Inca outpost. The Chiriguano attack was led by Aleixo Garcia, a Portuguese who had been shipwrecked on the coast of Brazil. Garcia was killed, but not before he was able to pass on the news of the fabulous kingdom of the Inca to other Europeans. Three years later, in 1527, an ailing Huayna Capac was greatly disturbed by reports of white men who had been seen sailing along the coast near Tumbes, a city in the northern part of his empire. But they sailed away again. Surprisingly enough, practically nothing had filtered through to Peru of the white man's exploits farther north, although Columbus had made his landfall in the New World 35 years earlier in 1492.

The Inca emperor had become increasingly attached to his northern district of Quito and had married a princess of the former Quito kingdom. He decided to break with tradition and leave four-fifths of his vast and somewhat unwieldy empire to Huáscar,

Above: genealogy from the late 1700's of Inca rulers and their Spanish successors. Manco Capac, the founder of the Inca dynasty, and his coya (official wife) stand in the two upper corners. The last of the Inca emperors, Atahualpa, and his successor, King Charles of Spain, are at the end of the second row.

Right: a gold funerary mask, decorated with emeralds from northern Peru. News of the Inca empire's great wealth brought the Spaniards to Peru as it had earlier drawn them to Mexico.

the legitimate heir, who was his principal wife's (his sister's) child. The remaining northern segment he left to Atahualpa, his son by the Quito princess. With this one action he called into question the inviolable rule governing the divine succession of the Inca. Nearly three years after his sudden death from illness in 1527, a civil war broke out as Huáscar and Atahualpa vied for total dominion of the Inca empire. The savage war lasted until 1532. Atahualpa's troops, which were made up of the best soldiers from Huayna Capac's army, eventually engaged Huáscar's forces several miles from Cuzco. The battle raged from dawn to dusk and resulted in victory for Atahualpa.

Atahualpa did not participate in the battle but remained at Cajamarca with reserve troops. During victory celebrations, word came that: "People have arrived by a big ship from out of the sea, with different clothing, beards, and animals like llamas, only larger." Atahualpa thought it wise to stay at his headquarters in Cajamarca, and delay his triumphant entry into Cuzco until he had met the strangers. Now that he had beaten his only rival to the throne, he was the most powerful man alive. The courier told him that there were less than 200 in the strange party approaching. If there was trouble, he could easily snuff them out.

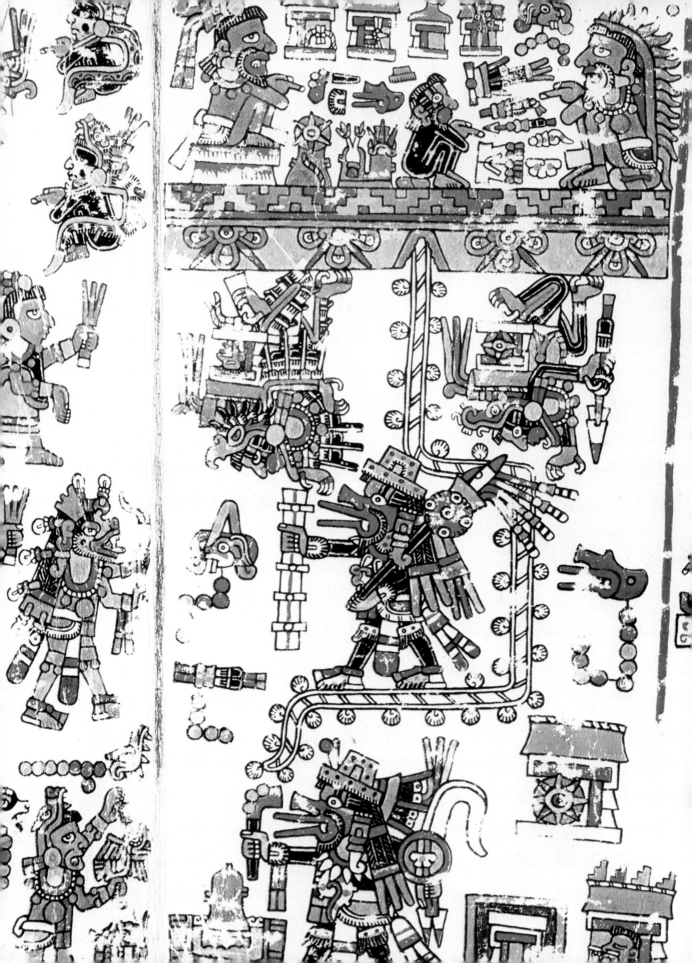

The Return of Quetzalcoatl

4

Above: portrait of Hernando Cortes at the time of the Spanish conquest by a Tlaxcalan artist. The conquistador is wearing a hat similar to that worn by the god Quetzalcoatl. The Mexican belief that Cortes was the god returning from exile was reinforced by the Spaniard's clothing and appearance.

News of the discovery of the New World by Christopher Columbus in 1492 surged through Europe with earth-shaking force. Nothing would ever be the same. The Renaissance, a rebirth of learning and culture that began in Italy in the 1300's, was now in full flower. An irresistible spirit of inquiry, speculative thought, and invention broadened man's horizons. There was a sharp increase in commerce. Man became eager to increase his knowledge of the world. Many time-honored assumptions could now be questioned. Columbus revealed that the habitable world was a much vaster place than ever conceived. Renaissance Europe was now offered the tantalizing prospect of spreading its new spirit of learning to distant lands.

In 1504, the same year that Columbus returned to Spain after his fourth expedition to the New World, a 19-year-old Spaniard by the name of Hernando Cortes arrived in Santo Domingo on the Caribbean island of Hispaniola (present-day Dominican Republic and Haiti). Cortes was in the vanguard of a new breed of conquistadors—explorers who were eager to earn personal glory and riches while opening up new kingdoms for the Spanish king.

In Hispaniola, Cortes discovered that the Spanish settlers were rapidly becoming disenchanted. Many of them had emigrated more than 10 years earlier to make their fortunes in the New World. The majority of settlers were obliged to earn a living by tilling the land. The only consolation—and that limited to those favored with the right connections—was a grant of land from which they could build up an estate, however modest, that would have been beyond their means in Spain.

Cortes became a popular figure in the small community. He showed courage in the irregular skirmishes with the Indians, and was "a great hand at games of cards and dice," enjoying himself whether winning or losing. He commanded an early following of people attracted to him because of his frankness and a disarming manner that rose above the trivia of island disputes.

For the next few years, Cortes was cast in the role of gentleman farmer, cultivating crops and raising horses and sheep. But his restless spirit yearned for more activity. The opportunity arose in 1511, when Diego Velásquez set out to conquer Cuba and Cortes promptly volunteered for service. After displaying his customary valor in subjugating the Cuban Indians, Cortes was given a choice of desirable property, to which he applied himself with some

Left: the giving of power to Quetzal-coatl as interpreted by an Indian artist. At the top of the picture, the bearded Quetzalcoatl sits among the temples and attributes being bestowed upon him by the heavens. In the lower part, he is seen descending to earth by means of a rope ladder. On his head he wears the high-crowned hat that was identified with the god.

Above: Indian slaves work at a Spanish sugar plantation on the island of Hispaniola. Spain's early colonies in the New World depended on Indian labor for both farming and mining.

industry. He made farming, mining, and livestock raising into a highly profitable undertaking. He was periodically in and out of favor with the corpulent Velásquez, who had been appointed first governor of Cuba. Cortes' reckless love affairs were disruptive to the new colony and he was suspected of intrigue against the person of the governor.

On February 8, 1517, Velásquez sent Francisco Hernández de Córdoba to explore the west and search for treasure. Once in the open sea, a furious storm drove Córdoba off course. Three weeks later he made landfall on an unfamiliar shoreline. Clambering on land, he and his men were astonished to see evidence of an Indian civilization that no one had till then imagined possible. Here were houses of stone and elaborately carved temples fashioned like pyramids. The inhabitants were colorfully dressed in finely woven cotton garments.

Córdoba had landed on the Yucatán Peninsula, directly west of

Cuba. There, the most brilliant of pre-Columbian American civilizations, the Maya, once held sway. Unlike the docile Arawak who inhabited the islands of the Caribbean, the mainland Indians were defiant. They drove Córdoba and his party away with a shower of stones and arrows. Rounding the cape of the peninsula and heading southwest to Campeche, a southeastern Mexican state, the party again encountered Indian hostility. Reluctantly, after suffering many casualties, Córdoba decided to return to Cuba, carrying with him some finely wrought specimens of gold.

The following year, on May 1, 1518, Velásquez sent out a second expedition to follow up Córdoba's discoveries. Under the command of Juan de Grijalva, the Spaniards sailed up the coast of the Yucatán Peninsula, rounded Cape Catoche and turned west into the Gulf of Mexico. Landing at Champoton, one of the cities where Córdoba's men had suffered heavy losses the year before, Grijalva beat off a strong attack from the inhabitants. He was as astounded as his predecessor had been by the stone temples and plazas, the large towns, and the fields of cultivated maize. Resuming his westward path he now ventured into areas beyond Córdoba's route. In what is today the state of Tabasco, he found Indians prepared to parley. From them he first heard of a land called Mexico, a powerful inland state where there was a plentiful supply of gold.

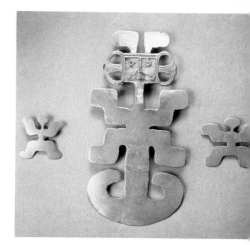

Above: gold ornament fashioned in the figure of a puma. Francisco de Córdoba carried similar samples of Maya goldwork back to Cuba where they excited official interest in the exploration of Mexico.

Left: Francisco de Córdoba's expedition sails along the coast of Yucatán after being blown off course by a storm. Córdoba was the first Spaniard to encounter traces of the Maya culture.

About 425 miles away, in Tenochtitlán, the Aztec capital of Mexico, Montezuma II had been following Grijalva's every move over the past month. Fleet-footed spies brought him details of the ships, the number of men-at-arms, and other descriptions by means of picture writing recorded on parchment. Montezuma was anxious to know more. These men answered in almost every detail the prophesied return of the god Quetzalcoatl. Their approach from the east, the beards, and the supernatural weapons of the Spaniards corresponded to Indian legend.

The prophesy said that Quetzalcoatl would return in the Aztec year Ce Acatl. This was to be 1519, the following year. Surely this was the god come to reclaim his throne. The utmost hospitality must be extended, and if fate so decreed, the benign deity might be pleased to delay his return until Montezuma, who was now middle aged, had concluded his reign.

The emperor sent a trusted chieftain and his slave to the coast to report personally on the strangers. Their news was disturbing: "... in the middle of the water [we saw] a house from which appeared white men, their faces white and their hands likewise. They have long thick beards and their clothing is of all colors: white, yellow, red, green, blue, and purple. On their heads they wear round coverings. They put a rather large canoe in the water, some of them jump into it and they fish all day near the rocks. At dusk they return to the home into which they are gathered. This is all we can tell you about that which you wish to know."

Montezuma instructed his two emissaries to return to the coast. This time they were told to make contact with the strangers and give them gold, precious stones, and some styled feather work. "If it is really Quetzalcoatl greet him on my behalf, and give him these gifts. You must also order the governor of Cuetlaztla to provide him with all kinds of food, cooked birds, and game. Let him also be given types of bread that are baked, together with fruit and gourds of chocolate." And, presumably as an acid test of identity, the emissaries were ordered to "notice very carefully whether he eats or not. If he eats and drinks he is surely Quetzalcoatl and this will show that he is familiar with the foods of this land, that he ate them once and has come back to savor them again." Then Montezuma concluded: "Also tell him to allow me to die. After my death he will be welcome to come here and take possession of his kingdom, as it is his. . . . Let

Above: Indian canoes attempt to capture one of Juan de Grijalva's ships in the Rio de Canoas. Grijalva explored the Yucatán coast as far as Tabasco where he first learned of the fabulous kingdom of Mexico.

Top left: Montezuma's emissaries carry gifts to the Spaniards.

Center left: the Indian ambassadors, unaccustomed to Spanish wine, "lost their sense" and were forced to spend the night aboard ship.

Left: the emissaries return to Montezuma with a gift of glass beads and report on the strange visitors and their ships, "more divine than human."

him permit me to end my days here. Then let him return to enjoy what is his!"

Shortly before dawn of the next day, the gifts and food were laid down on the beach and the two envoys waited for sunrise and the Spaniards. When Grijalva saw the Mexicans, he invited them aboard ship. The cabins and the rigging seemed to the Indians, "a thing more divine than human." The Spaniards thoroughly enjoyed the strange food. With "much laughing and sporting," they became the first Europeans to feast on turkey and chocolate. These must have been doubly welcome as Grijalva was nearing the end of his journey, and his supplies were low. Not to be outdone in hospitality, they offered the Indians the rather unappetizing ships' rations of jerked beef, bacon, and stale biscuits. Then Grijalva offered them some wine and after the first sip "their hearts were gladdened." But being unaccustomed to it, they "lost their sense" and had to spend the night aboard ship to recover. Before sailing away, the strangers intimated by sign language that they would return. In parting they gave the Mexicans a necklace to present to their sovereign.

The emissaries returned to Tenochtitlán and presented Montezuma with the necklace of glass beads, which he mistook for precious stones. Then they offered him the biscuit that the gods had given them. The king tasted it and said it was like tufa stone—a calcium carbonate deposit often found in river beds. He sent for a piece of the latter and solemnly weighed one against the other, discovering that the rock weighed less. He then summoned his dwarfs to taste it. Finally, Montezuma claimed that he was afraid to eat it as it

Left: the Aztec emperor, Montezuma, as pictured by a Spanish artist in the late 1600's. The crowned ruler is seen surrounded by the wealth and splendor of the Aztec empire, as he is borne by his nobles through the streets of Tenochtitlán.

"belonged to the gods and it would be sacrilege." The priests were instructed to bury it outside city limits. With due ceremony the biscuit was transported to Tula (or Tollan), ancient capital of the earlier Toltec civilization, where it was buried at the temple of Quetzalcoatl. On learning of the strangers' intended return, all the thinly suppressed fears, anxieties, and conflicting emotions returned to Montezuma. He needed no more reassurance that the god Quetzalcoatl was indeed returning on the scheduled date.

After naming the region he had explored *New Spain*, Grijalva returned to Cuba with samples of gold and stories of greater treas-

Above: the Temple of Quetzalcoatl at Tula, the ancient capital of the Toltec civilization. Believing that the biscuit sent to him by Grijalva "belonged to the gods." Montezuma ordered it to be carried to Tula and buried.

Right: portrait of Diego Velásquez and a view of the coast of Cuba, which he conquered in 1511. As governor of Cuba, Velásquez befriended the young Cortes and gave him command of an expedition to conquer Mexico. Below: Cortes' fleet sails to Mexico. The conquistador fell out of favor with Velásquez, but sailed clandestinely before the governor could revoke his commission. After recruiting additional men and supplies along the coast of Cuba, Cortes embarked for the mainland.

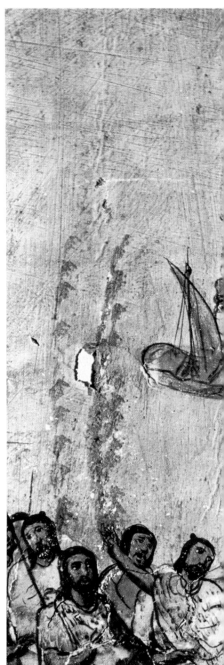

ures. Instead of a hero's welcome, Grijalva was subjected to a torrent of abuse from Velásquez. The governor was furious that he had adhered so rigidly to his instructions and had not established a settlement in the territory of his new discoveries.

Now that the rumor of a fabulous kingdom to the west bore some measure of authenticity, Governor Velásquez was anxious to stake his claim before others got around to it. He hurried preparations for a new, much larger, expeditionary force, while casting an eye around for someone to head it. His choice fell on his former secretary, Cortes, who had been waiting for just such an opportunity. By mortgaging his property, Cortes contributed the bulk of the cost of outfitting the expedition. Velásquez advanced the remainder. Soon, however, the unpredictable Velásquez thought he detected a change in his protégé's demeanor. He predicted with absolute certainty that Cortes would flout his authority. Velásquez was encouraged in this belief by relatives and others who coveted Cortes' command.

Cortes was warned that Velásquez was seriously considering an alternative choice to lead the expedition. But before his appointment could be revoked, Cortes led his tiny fleet clandestinely out of Santiago de Cuba harbor on the southern coast of Cuba. He spent the next couple of months sailing along the coast of Cuba, picking up more recruits and supplies while ignoring Valásquez' summons to return. At last all was ready. On February 18, 1519, Cortes set sail with a force of about 550 soldiers, 11 ships, 16 horses, 10 brass guns, and 4 small cannons, called falconets.

Cortes headed for Cozumel Island off the coast of Yucatán. When he arrived, he discovered that several of his party had landed before him and had robbed the Indians of much of their possessions. Incensed at this irresponsible behavior, he upbraided the leader, the headstrong Pedro de Alvarado, and ordered all the looted goods be returned to the Indians. "We should never pacify the country in that way by robbing Indians of their property," Cortes declared.

Cortes was always at pains to adhere to proper diplomatic preliminaries. On Cozumel, his first act was to order the reading of the *requerimento* to the Indians. This was a rarely understood document from the King of Spain that invited Indians to become subjects of Spain and take up the true faith in peace. If they refused, the document ordered that "war shall be made on them with fire and sword,

Salen tres navios de Santiago de Cuba
a descubrir

A

and they shall be killed and enslaved." Before leaving the island, Cortes rescued a Spanish castaway, Jeronimo de Aguilar, who had been a slave to an Indian *cacique* (chieftain) for the past eight years. As Aguilar was fluent in the Maya tongue, he became a welcome addition to the party as an interpreter. Continuing his journey of exploration, Cortes headed for Tabasco, the spot where Grijalva had met with friendly Indians the year before. But on this occasion the Spaniards' overtures were met with a rebuff. The Tabascans had been taunted by their neighbors for their cowardly behavior in not

Left: Malinche, an Indian princess who became Cortes' translator, interprets the words of a Mexican cacique to the conquistador. Called *Dona Marina* by the Spaniards, Malinche was presented to Cortes as part of the spoils from the battle of Tabasco. She became his loyal and devoted mistress.

Left: "Battle of Tabasco," by an unknown Spanish artist in the 1600's. Cortes and his men were met with angry defiance when they landed on the coast of Tabasco. In his first major battle on Mexican soil, the conquistador demonstrated his skill as a strategist by defeating an Indian army that outnumbered his forces by 22 to 1.

HERNAN CORES

Above: perhaps the most authentic likeness of Cortes, this drawing was made by Franz Weiditz in the 1500's. Weiditz is believed to have met the conqueror in Spain several years after the conquest of Mexico.

Left: portrait by an unknown artist of Hernando Cortes as a young man. This heroic likeness, painted many years after the conquistador's death, presents an idealized picture of what the conqueror of Mexico looked like.

attacking Grijalva's party. Fighting broke out and 12,000 Tabascan warriors took the field, outnumbering Cortes' small force 22 to 1. However, superior tactics together with advantages of musket, cannon, and steel sword prevailed over native spear, lance, and sling. The battle is vividly described by Bernard Diaz del Castillo, a member of Cortes' expedition who wrote an eyewitness account of the Spanish conquest of Mexico. "I remember," says Diaz, "that when we fired shots the Indians gave great shouts and whistles and threw dust and rubbish into the air so that we should not see the danger done to them, and they sounded their trumpets and drums and shouted and whistled and cried 'Alala! Alala!' " But the cavalry terminated the conflict abruptly. "Just at this time we caught sight of our horsemen," continues Diaz, "and as the great Indian host was crazed with its attack on us, it did not at once perceive them coming up behind their backs . . . they came quickly on the enemy and speared them as they chose. As soon as we saw the horsemen we fell on the Indians with such energy that with us attacking on one side and the horsemen on the other, they soon turned tail. The Indians thought that the horse and its rider was all one animal, for they had never seen horses up to this time."

The battle was won by the Spaniards. The caciques swore allegiance to the Spanish king and became Christian subjects. Food, gold, and other treasures were then brought to the victors. Among the valuable gifts presented to Cortes were 20 Tabascan girls. One of them, called Malinche, became his devoted and loyal mistress and later bore him a son, Don Martin Cortes. Diaz recalls that the Spaniards christened her Dona Marina, because "she was truly a great chieftainess and the daughter of great Caciques. . . ." Malinche spoke both *Nahuatl*, the Aztec language, and *Mayan*, the language Aguilar knew. Between the two of them, Cortes now had an interpreting team that could enable him to make contact wherever he went. Soon, the bright Malinche picked up Spanish and replaced Aguilar as Cortes' mouthpiece. Cortes was to rely more and more on her other qualities, her tact and counsel, which he was wise enough to heed from the start.

Cortes now continued along the coast until he reached a point on the coast near the island of San Juan de Ulua. Montezuma, anticipating Quetzalcoatl's return, had dispatched emissaries to the coast days earlier. They were waiting to greet the returning god. When the

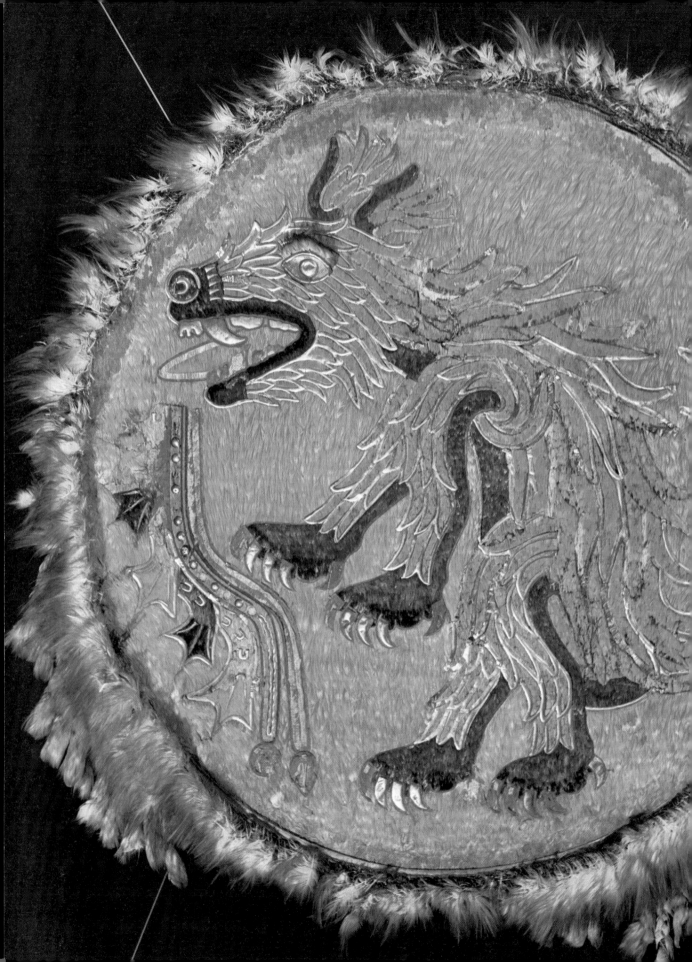

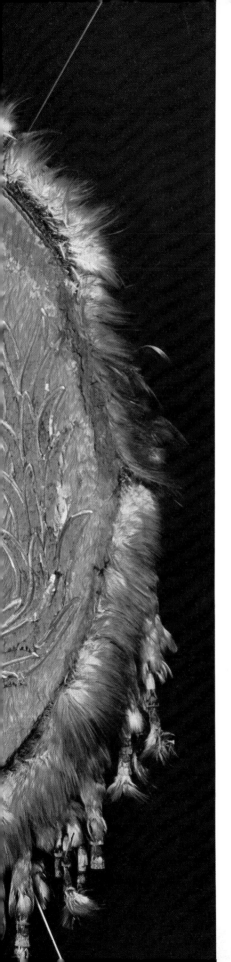

Left: an Aztec warrior's shield, adorned
with an elaborate feather mosaic depicting a prairie wolf. It was sent to Spain
as a gift to the bishop of Palencia, in
the early 1500's. Similar gifts, showing
the exquisite craftsmanship of the Aztec
were sent to the Spanish king. Both
Church and monarchy had an intense
interest in the conquest of the Americas:
priests were sent to convert the Indians
to Christianity; conquistadors
were sent to fill the king's coffers.

Spaniards appeared, the Mexicans went aboard and welcomed Cortes
in the name of their emperor. On Friday, April 21, 1519, Cortes gave
the order to disembark on the mainland. By an extraordinary coincidence, he had landed not only in the same year and month as
Quetzalcoatl promised to return, but also on the very day named by
the prophecy. The person who was the least surprised by this time
was Montezuma. Since Grijalva's appearance the previous year, the
Aztec emperor had been convinced that the deity would arrive at the
appointed hour.

Montezuma was in a quandary: to which of the two major gods
should he turn? Should he choose Quetzalcoatl, the gentle deity who
eschewed human sacrifice, or the god of war and sun, Huitzilopochtli, who demanded incessant human sacrifice and who had driven
out Quetzalcoatl? After much soul-searching and numerous con-
sultations with his ministers, priests, and soothsayers, Montezuma
decided he could not risk offending either god. Least of all, as emperor of the Chosen People of the Sun, could he afford to offend
their ancient tribal deity, Huitzilopochtli. Accordingly, he decided to
lavish goods on the god Quetzalcoatl whom he saw in the person of
Cortes. If not remorselessly bent on revenge, Quetzalcoatl might be
persuaded to leave.

When Cortes received the gifts intended for Quetzalcoatl he was
astonished at the treasures of which he was now the proud possessor.
As he did not yet understand the significance of these offerings, he
was overwhelmed by the generosity of the emperor. "The first
article presented was a wheel like a sun, as big as a cartwheel, with
many sorts of pictures on it, the whole of fine gold, and a wonderful
thing to behold, which those who afterwards weighed it said was
worth more than $10,000. Then another wheel was presented of
greater size made of silver of great brilliancy in imitation of the moon
with other figures shown on it, and this was of great value as it was
very heavy."

The royal gifts that were intended to hasten Quetzalcoatl's
departure had the reverse effect on Cortes. Nothing would be toler-
ated that stood in the way of his coming face-to-face with his ad-
versary. "I intended," he wrote to his king, "to advance and see him
wherever he might be found," and vowed he "would bring him
either dead or in chains if he would not submit . . . to your Majesty's
crown."

The Fall of Tenochtitlán
5

Cortes and his men had landed on a melancholy strip of the Mexican coast. They called the low, sandy, mosquito-ridden area *Tierra Caliente* (literally, hot land). The army suffered severely from the hot, fetid swamps. Thirty-five men died, either from tropical fever or from wounds received at Tabasco. A move became necessary, either to a more attractive spot in Mexico or back to Cuba. Cortes not only refused to return to Cuba, but he had himself elected captain and chief justice of a new colony, and the municipality of Veracruz, the first of its kind in New Spain, henceforth recognized the authority of none but the King of Spain (who as Charles V, was elected Holy Roman

Above: arrival of Cortes at Veracruz. Spanish horsemen gallop along the beach to the roar of cannons. In the upper left-hand corner, a delegation of ambassadors from Montezuma witnesses the landing of the Spanish forces.

Emperor in 1519). Cortes was careful to preserve the appearance of legality in his usurpation of Velásquez' control. He sent one of his ships back to Spain with a letter to the king explaining his action. He reinforced his claim by turning over the entire treasure he had received from Montezuma to the king.

Cortes was determined to march on the Aztec capital. To make certain that others would share his resolve he sank all but one of his ships. Thus he removed the last opportunity for the fainthearted to return to Cuba. In the meantime he had been visited by emissaries from a cacique of the Totonac federation of cities in the area. They

A.

B.

complained of the intolerable burden of being a vassal state of the Aztec and asked for help against their oppressors. Diaz notes Cortes' reaction to this request. "As he stood there thinking the matter over, he said laughingly to some of us companions who were with him: 'Do you know, gentlemen, that it seems to me that we have already gained a great reputation for valor throughout this country . . . the people here take us for gods or beings like their idols.' "

The shrewd Cortes, preposterously outnumbered, now had the germ of a solution to Montezuma's vulnerability. If the Totonac Indians were smoldering with discontent, there might be many other tribute-paying states of similar disposition. Under his direction these combined forces could topple Montezuma and his loosely-knit empire. With an army consisting of 400 men, 15 horses, and 6 cannon, Cortes set off on the first leg of his 200-mile march to the Aztec capital. A small garrison was detailed to guard the new settlement at Veracruz. At Cempoala, the Totonac capital, the cacique provided the Spaniards with 200 porters and "40 chieftains, all warriors." The cacique advised Cortes to pass through Tlaxcala, where the inhabitants, hostile to the Aztec, might prove allies.

Above: the sinking of the fleet that had carried Cortes and his men to Mexico. Before setting out for the interior, Cortes gave the command for the ships to be scuttled. The conquistador was "determined to make my way in this land or die here."

Below: the Tlaxcalan sue for peace. After a fierce battle, Cortes defeated the Tlaxcalan army and made an alliance with them against the Aztec. The Tlaxcalan were to prove themselves the most steadfast and loyal of the Spaniards' Indian allies.

The Spaniards left Cempoala in mid-August of 1519, and two weeks later crossed the borders into Tlaxcala. The Tlaxcalan Indians had never been subjugated by the Aztec. Cortes' dealings with Montezuma's emissaries and the Aztec vassal state of the Totonac, made the Tlaxcalan suspicious. Their attitude was blunt: "We will kill those *teules* (gods) and eat their flesh." And they attacked without negotiation.

There is no doubt that Cortes' tiny force was hopelessly outnumbered and this time they were faced by a people who were more warlike than the coastal tribes, and who made more effective use of their weaponry. They were particularly adept with the spear thrower, which, in the hands of a skilled warrior, was a devastating weapon.

During a lull in the fighting, 50 envoys of the Tlaxcalan came to the camp, ostensibly on a peace-making mission. When interrogated separately, they confessed to being spies. Cortes returned them all to their chieftains with their hands cut off. The fighting continued and the Spaniards were again victorious. The Indians submitted to Cortes, acknowledging: "We have done all we could to kill you and your companions, but our gods are worthless against you. We have determined to be your friends and serve you, and because in this province we are surrounded on all sides by our enemies, we beg you to protect us against them, and to come to our city of Tlaxcala to rest from the labors we have given you." The addition of the Tlaxcalan army was the turning point in Cortes' fortunes. Through all times, whether good or bad, he could not have found more steadfast allies.

It was while at Tlaxcala that Cortes heard from Montezuma again. This time Montezuma invited the Spaniards to come to Tenochtitlán, and suggested that they pass through Cholula on the way. Cholula was the sacred city of Quetzalcoatl. In addition to 400 temples, the city boasted a pyramid larger than the Great Pyramid in Egypt. Cortes' Tlaxcalan allies warned him that the Cholula route was a trap. When Cortes insisted that he would go anyway, he was given a bodyguard of 6,000 warriors.

Now only Cholula lay between Cortes and his ultimate goal, Tenochtitlán, 80 miles distant. The Cholulan who came out to greet him took exception to the presence of their sworn foes, the Tlaxcalan. Cortes ordered his allies to stay beyond the outskirts of the city while he and his men retired to quarters in the main temple precincts. After several days Malinche warned Cortes of a plot to wipe out the Spaniards. Cortes reacted quickly. He invited the city's warriors, caciques, and other leading dignitaries into the temple enclosure. At a given signal, the unarmed Cholulan were fired upon and then put to the sword.

The road now lay open to Tenochtitlán. One week and 60 miles separated Cortes from Montezuma. By this time, nearly all the Spaniards shared their leader's enthusiasm to complete the historic journey. Cortes turned down the offer of a fighting force of 10,000 Tlaxcalan warriors, requesting instead that 1,000 Indians accompany the Spaniards as porters.

Below: massacre of Indians at Cholula. This watercolor shows both men and women being beaten and killed while struggling under the heavy burden of the Spaniards' luggage. Cortes ordered the massacre as punishment for a supposed Indian plot against the lives of the Spanish soldiers.

Above: valley of the Pasa Cortes through which Cortes marched on his way to Tenochtitlán. The pass lies between the twin volcanoes, left, Popocatépetl (smoking mountain) and, right, Ixtacihuatl (white woman).
Below: an Indian artist depicts Cortes' forces emerging from the Pasa Cortes into the Valley of Mexico.

On November 1, 1519, the army took its leave of Cholula, a city in mourning. Towering before them, 20 miles distant, were the famous volcanoes, Popocatépetl (*smoking mountain*), and the two-breasted Ixtacihuatl (*white woman*). Cortes' route lay directly between the two giant snow-capped mountains, both soaring skyward to a height of over 17,000 feet above sea level. Slicing through the pine trees, icy gusts of wind swept down the mountain slopes as the army climbed higher up the rugged terrain. The battle-hardened soldiers shivered in their cotton-quilted jackets. The horses became unnerved. Ice, snow, and sleet slowed them to a crawl. When dusk fell, Cortes ordered his men to halt for the night. They camped about six miles short of the top of the pass.

The next morning they continued to the top. Crossing the last ridge, the Spaniards stopped short and gazed in awe at the spectacle confronting them. Below, thirty cities were evenly sprinkled in all directions. The jewel of all was the island-city of Tenochtitlán. Its gleaming white temples and white plastered houses were interspersed with trees and surrounded by the shimmering blue waters of Lake Texcoco. Their wonder increasing at every step, the Spaniards made their way to the gates of Tenochtitlán.

Montezuma came out to meet the Spaniards. Nobles lined the sides of a broad avenue as Montezuma was borne past on a golden, jewel-

Above: The Old World meets the New. A Spanish painting of the 1600's shows the epic confrontation between Cortes and Montezuma—the explorer dressed in the armor of medieval Europe and the emperor of the Aztec clothed in the riches of Mexico.

studded litter. A green canopy, decorated with tail feathers of the sacred Quetzal bird, shaded the emperor from the sun. Courtiers swept the ground, laying down cotton cloths before the path of the royal litter. The nobles averted their eyes as the emperor passed, not daring to look him in the face as he readied to greet the heavensent strangers from across the sea. Montezuma was richly attired. While his nobles went barefoot, the emperor wore gold sandals encrusted with precious stones.

Cortes and Montezuma at last met face-to-face. The Mexican version of this historic confrontation is recorded in Bernardino de Sahagún's *General History of the Things of New Spain*.

" 'Is it true that you are the king Montezuma?' asked Cortes. And the king said: 'Yes I am Montezuma.' Then he stood up to welcome Cortes; he came forward, bowed his head low and addressed him in

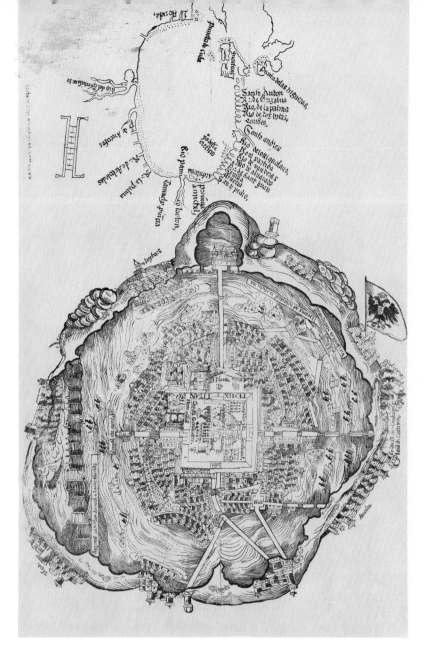

Above: map of the city of Tenochtitlán
made under the supervision of Cortes.
It shows the three main causeways
leading into the city. At the center
is an enlargement of the temple area—
the heart of the Aztec capital.

these words: 'Our lord, you are weary. The journey has tired you, but now you have arrived on earth. You have come to your city, Mexico. You have come back to sit on your throne, to sit under its canopy. The kings who have gone before, your representatives, guarded it and preserved it for your coming. . . . Do the kings know the destiny of those they left behind, their posterity? If only they are watching! If only they can see what I see! No, it is in my dreams. . . . I have seen you at last! I have met you face to face! I was in agony for five days, for ten days, with my eyes fixed on the Region of Mystery. And now you have come out of the clouds and mists to sit on your throne again. This was foretold by the kings who governed your city, and now it has taken place. You have come back to us; you have come down from the sky. Rest now, and take possession of your royal houses. Welcome to your land, my lords!'

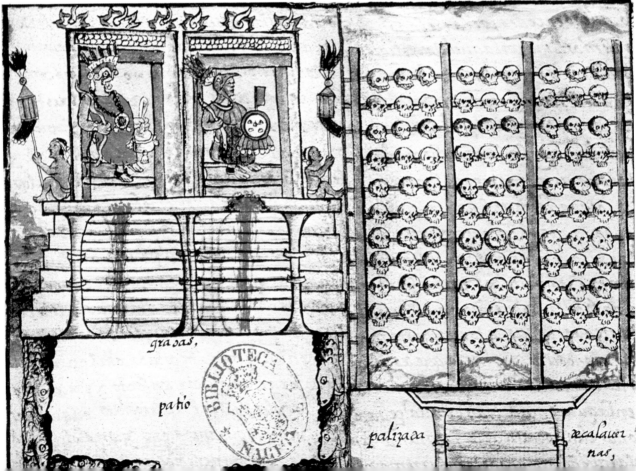

graias,

patio

palizaa

æcalauer
nas,

"Cortes replied: 'Tell Montezuma that we are his friends. There is nothing to fear. We have wanted to see him for a long time, and now we have seen his face and heard his words. Tell him that we love him and that our hearts are contented.' "

The Spaniards were housed in a magnificent palace fronting the main plaza of Tenochtitlán. The temple of Huitzilopochtli that dominated the city separated the newcomers from the emperor's palace. Here, each day, the Spaniards were obliged to witness the horrors of human sacrifice. The dead victim, his heart excised, was hurled from the top of the temple. Choice limbs were saved for the repasts of priests and nobles while the torsos were tossed to the hungry beasts in the adjoining zoo. A skull rack, called a *tzompantli,* stood nearby. It contained 136,000 human skulls—victims of this religious sacrifice.

Cortes was treated graciously by Montezuma, but was always on the alert. Despite the hospitality of his host, he disliked the idea that his very existence hung on the slender thread of the emperor's caprice. And although Montezuma seemed well disposed at the moment, he could easily change his mind. After one week, Cortes decided on a daring maneuver: He would take the emperor prisoner and at once achieve dominion over the Aztec. Montezuma would remain as ruler in name only, a puppet-king.

To accomplish this bold plan, Cortes took 30 armed soldiers, his most trusted captains, and the loyal Malinche, to the emperor's palace. He declared that he had come to take the emperor to his lodgings for surveillance. At first the emperor was incredulous that anyone—god or not god—could behave with such audacity. But Malinche's quiet insistence that he would be killed on the spot unless he complied stopped all further remonstrations on his part. The emperor was borne away on his litter, seemingly resigned to his fate, while vainly attempting to reassure his weeping nobles that all was well and everything would be back to normal shortly. Though Cortes encouraged Montezuma to conduct government business from his new domicile, the emperor suffered no illusions that his status was anything but a crude version of house arrest. His subjects, unused to acting without a leader, were stunned into submission. Montezuma was made to undergo a ceremony as humiliating to his councilors as the abduction from the royal palace. He was forced to swear allegiance to the Spanish king.

Above: Montezuma, in captivity, receives Cortes and his officers. Although surrounded by the semblance of power, Montezuma was reduced to the status of a puppet ruler and forced to swear allegiance to the Spanish king.

One day Cortes, struck by the priests' insolent mocking of his explanations of Christianity, could contain his evangelical wrath no longer. "Oh God! Why do you permit such great honor paid the Devil in this land? Oh Lord, it is good that we are here to serve you." An eyewitness account then describes what followed, as Cortes addressed the temple priests. " 'It will give me great pleasure to fight for my God against your gods, who are a mere nothing.' Before the men he had sent for arrived, Cortes took up an iron bar that was there and began to smash the stone idols."

With this single action, Cortes dashed all hopes of ever gaining the Aztec empire by peaceful means. He had undone the incredible gains he had achieved by skill, courage, diplomacy, guile, and luck. He had committed the unpardonable sin of meddling with the gods who controlled the cosmic forces. Each blow delivered at Huitzilo-pochtli struck at the very core of Aztec belief. Montezuma, horrified at Cortes' sacriligious excess, and brooking no further nonsense on this score, warned that he had only to lift one finger and the whole populace would storm the building. Cortes believed him. As the

Above: Montezuma leads the Spaniards to the treasure of the Aztec kings. A contemporary account of the conquest states that in their search for gold, the Spaniards "did not leave a corner or chamber unsearched or undisturbed." Below left: besieged by Aztec warriors, Alvarado and his men seek refuge in their quarters after brutally massacring unarmed Aztec men during a religious festival.

priests were already inciting the people to rebellion, Montezuma continued, the Spaniards' only chance of survival was to leave the city immediately.

With the Aztec on the point of uprising, events now took a turn for the worse from an unexpected quarter. A messenger on the coast reported that a substantial force had arrived from Cuba to overthrow the rebels. The situation was dangerous because many of Cortes' soldiers were in distant provinces collecting gold. Leaving Alvarado in charge at Tenochtitlán, Cortes set out with 82 men to Cempoala where the Cuban force was encamped. Under the twin covers of night and a heavy rainfall, Cortes' men took the rebels by surprise and defeated them. Cortes had only a few moments, however, to enjoy his victory. Messengers brought the news that Alvarado was besieged in the capital.

During Cortes' absence Alvarado had given permission for the Mexicans to celebrate the solemn feast of Toxcatl, during which the idol of Huitzilopochtli was moved from one temple to another. On

the day of the feast, thousands of Aztec men, unarmed and dressed only in rich plumes and precious jewels, gathered in the city's main square to begin a ritual dance. Whether in fear of so large an assemblage of warriors, or aroused by the great wealth that adorned the dancers, Alvarado gave his soldiers the signal to attack. The brutal massacre that followed has been called "the most atrocious act ever committed in this land: the end of the flower and nobility of Mexico." Alvarado and his men took refuge in the palace where they were besieged by the outraged population of Tenochtitlán.

When Cortes returned to Tenochtitlán, the city was deathly still. On the whole, Cortes was in a good frame of mind. He had not had to fight his way back into the capital as expected. Many soldiers from the Cuban force had defected to Cortes, and strengthened the Spanish army threefold. Having achieved the near impossible with but 400 men, Cortes felt confident he could handle almost any crisis from now on. But what he failed to understand was that the one man who could guarantee his immunity was now powerless. The high council was already deliberating on a successor to Montezuma.

Below: from the roof of his palace, Montezuma begs the Aztec to make peace with the Spaniards. Roused to fever pitch, the Indians responded with a hail of arrows and stones, one of which is believed to have fatally wounded the Aztec emperor.

In an attempt to negotiate the reopening of the market, Cortes released from custody the emperor's brother Cuitlahuac. Unwittingly, he had provided the Aztec with their next leader. Led by Cuitlahuac, the Aztec attacked the following day. The Spaniards were surprised at the fury of their assailants. "Neither cannon nor muskets nor crossbows availed, nor hand-to-hand fighting, nor killing 30 or 40 of them every time we charged, for they still fought on in as close ranks and with more energy than in the beginning. . . ." noted Diaz, the Spanish commentator.

On the third day of hostilities, Cortes summoned Montezuma to address his people, giving the assurance that the Spaniards would leave if granted safe conduct out of the city. Montezuma reluctantly agreed to appeal to his people but knew in his own heart that it would be useless. His authority had been transferred to his brother, Cuitlahuac. For this event, he dressed himself in his imperial robes. All fighting ceased when he stood on the palace rooftop. His presence still commanded a respectful silence. But as soon as reference was made to the Spaniards, who stood on either side of him there arose an angry roar. A volley of arrows, stones, and darts was let loose at the odious intruders. Montezuma was struck by three stones, one on the temple wounding him fatally.

Cortes realized that his chances of survival were growing slimmer the longer he stayed in the capital. The only alternative was to attempt a breakthrough to the mainland. The shortest route was to the west to Tacuba, a distance of only two miles. The causeway, however, was linked by three bridges that had all been removed. Cortes ordered the construction of a portable bridge, with the idea of transporting it to cover the gaps as they advanced. On the day Montezuma died, Cortes drew up his final plans.

Shortly before midnight, on June 30, 1520, afterward known as *La Noche Triste,* the army stole out of the palace. Under the cover of darkness the Spaniards crossed the deserted city. The alarm was soon sounded. Priests banged on snake drums, and the great booming sounds reverberated throughout the valley. Suddenly the city came alive. The lake was a mass of canoes speeding toward the causeway to cut off the escape route. The portable bridge had to be abandoned. By now arrows, stones, darts, and javelins were hurled from canoes. Plunging down off the side of the causeway, the lucky Spaniards drowned, the others screamed as they were hauled off for sacrifice. Swords hacked through flesh. The yells, whistles, and shrieks were deafening. Carcasses of horses, human bodies, cannon, and treasure formed the inanimate bridge over which the soldiers passed from one gap to the next. Cortes was now on the mainland, and like the others, streaming blood from his wounds. Malinche, too, was safe.

But Alvarado and the rear section were in trouble. Cortes galloped back and plunged into a sea of canoes. Struggling on to the causeway and across the next gap, he saw his comrade on the other side. Alvarado was surrounded by the enemy. The Aztec recognized with glee the man they had nicknamed *Tonatio* (the sun). Suddenly,

Above: on June 30, 1520, Cortes and his men began their retreat from the Aztec capital. The Spaniards called it *La Noche Triste,* "the sad night," because so many of their number perished at the hands of frenzied Aztec warriors. The streets and canals of Tenochtitlán were choked with the mangled bodies of men and horses. According to one Spanish chronicler, on that night "Cortes lost seven hundred men, all of them cut to pieces mercilessly."

Left: Indian drawing showing Spanish soldiers tossing the bodies of Montezuma and one of his chiefs into a canal. Many Aztec sources claim that Montezuma was murdered by the Spaniards, and not by his own people.

Alvarado took his lance, plunged it into the melee of bodies and canoes, and vaulted to safety. Together, Alvarado and Cortes fought their way back to the mainland. The gray light of dawn exposed the wreckage of their flight. While his army regrouped, Cortes looked back toward the city and saw the utter desolation left in their trail. More than two-thirds of his force was destroyed. He turned and wept sad, bitter tears, under a cypress tree, *El Arbol de la Noche Triste,* which still stands in this sector of Mexico City to commemorate the incident.

The Spaniards' troubles, however, were far from over. They had more than 100 miles of Aztec territory to cross before reaching Tlaxcala, the land of their allies. Cortes rallied his men, although all were drained of energy through hunger and exertion. After a final clash with the Aztec forces, during which they overcame incredible odds, the Spaniards crossed into Tlaxcalan territory.

They received a warm welcome from their allies, whose admiration for the white strangers was further increased by their having escaped with their lives from the island-fortress of Tenochtitlán.

Cortes immediately began to make preparations for an all-out assault on the Aztec capital. Ten months later he was ready. In May, 1521, he attacked Tenochtitlán, his tactic being to lay siege to the city in the lake by severing its links with the mainland. To achieve this involuntary embargo that would prevent canoes bringing merchandise to the island, he built brigantines (small vessels) and at once gained control of the lake. Then he cut off the fresh water supply from Chapultepec. Now followed the most ferocious fighting of the Spanish incursion into the New World as the courageous Aztec defended their city to the last man, preferring death to surrender.

For 80 days the Aztec held out as one by one the beautiful buildings, palaces, and houses were razed to the ground. Montezuma's 22-year-old nephew, Cuauhtémoc, was now the emperor. (Cuitlahuac had died of smallpox after reigning only four months). Cortes was nearly captured on two occasions but managed to escape the fate reserved for his less fortunate comrades, who every day were offered to the gods. The ominous sound of the snake drum would signal the commencement of this ghastly rite, the platform above the temple steps elevated so as to be in full view of the watching conquistadors. The captive Spaniard, adorned in feathers, was made

Right: Cortes began his seige of Tenochtitlán in May of 1521. Refusing to surrender to the Spaniards, the Aztec saw their city burned to the ground. In this drawing from the Codex Azcatitlan, Indian warriors are seen defending the sacred temple —the last Aztec stronghold.

Below: capture of Cuauhtémoc, last emperor of the Aztec. According to Indian history, Cuauhtémoc begged his captors to "tell the captain [Cortes] that I have done my duty. . . . But I have failed. Now that I am his captive, let him take this dagger and kill me with it."

to perform a grotesque dance in front of the idols before he was stretched over the sacrificial stone.

But in the surrounded city of Tenochtitlán itself, conditions were wretched beyond belief. Disease ravaged the entire island community. Cortes begged the Aztec to surrender, but Cuauhtémoc still would not give in. "I know not how to free ourselves without destroying their city—the most beautiful city in the world . . . we found them more undaunted than ever . . . the plan was to demolish every house as we penetrated into the city and not to advance a step until all was level with the ground." Finally, on August 13, 1521, Cuauhtémoc was captured. The city was in ruins except for a small enclave around the market precinct of Tlatelolco. Women and children clawed their way across the causeways, swaying and collapsing, to strip the trees for bark, or grovel in the ground for insects or worms, anything to satisfy their desperate pangs of hunger. Nothing but masonry rubble remained to remind the onlooker of the glories of the Aztec past.

Cortes began to rebuild the city. He erected a cathedral on the site where the temple of Huitzilopochtli with its sacrificial altar had stood. Fourteen months later, his titles and honors were confirmed by the Spanish king. He was appointed governor and captain general of New Spain. He devoted his energies to making the Mexican empire a model Spanish colony. Cattle and plants were imported from Europe. Spaniards were allocated estates, but Cortes was vigilant that abuses accorded the Caribbean Indians should not be repeated in New Spain. Tribes that cooperated with the new government were treated with consideration. The rest were subjugated ruthlessly.

Cortes' captains opened up territories beyond the boundaries of the old Aztec empire. Pedro de Alvarado penetrated deep into the south, and after three years subdued the highland Maya. As a reward, he was given the governorship of Guatemala. Cristóbal de Olid, a captain in Cortes' army, was sent to Honduras. After penetrating

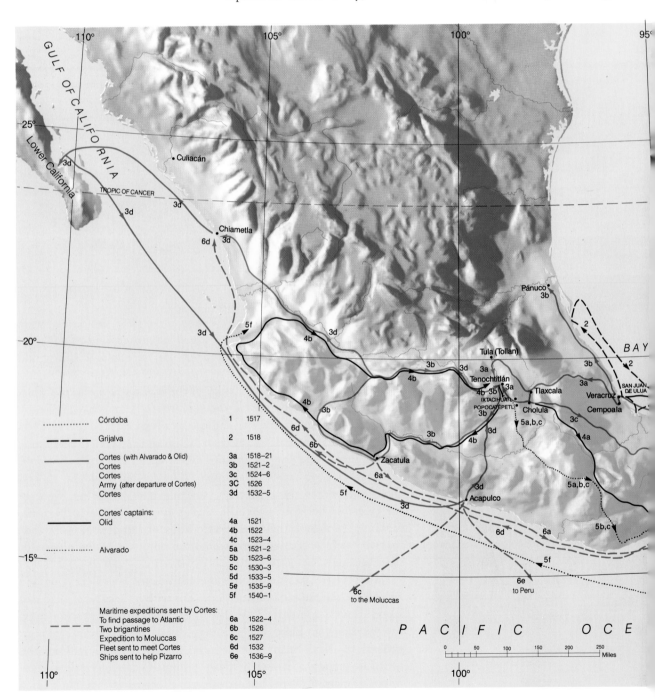

·········· Córdoba	1	1517
– – – Grijalva	2	1518
——— Cortes (with Alvarado & Olid)	3a	1518–21
Cortes	3b	1521–2
Cortes	3c	1524–6
Army (after departure of Cortes)	3C	1526
Cortes	3d	1532–5
Cortes' captains:		
Olid	4a	1521
	4b	1522
	4c	1523–4
	5a	1521–2
	5b	1523–6
·········· Alvarado	5c	1530–3
	5d	1533–5
	5e	1535–9
	5f	1540–1
Maritime expeditions sent by Cortes:		
– – – To find passage to Atlantic	6a	1522–4
Two brigantines	6b	1526
Expedition to Moluccas	6c	1527
Fleet sent to meet Cortes	6d	1532
Ships sent to help Pizarro	6e	1536–9

Honduras, he promptly disavowed Cortes. In an achievement some rank as phenomenal as the conquest of Mexico, Cortes marched 1,300 miles overland in pursuit of Olid. He had to negotiate a terrain of unimaginable difficulty, tropical forest, fever-ridden swamp, and range upon range of mountains. Olid paid for his mutiny on the executioner's block. Cortes was away from the capital for just under two years. After he returned, he equipped several maritime expeditions along the Pacific coast, to search for a strait to the Spice Islands, and in the process discovered what is now Lower California. The land

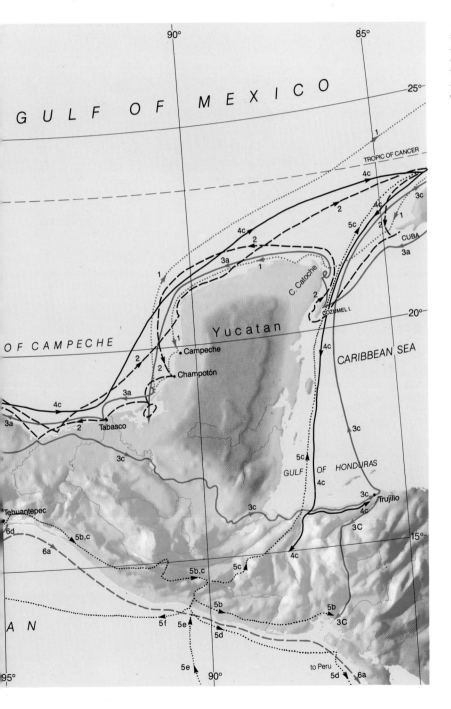

Left: this map of what is now Mexico shows the movements of Cortes and his armies and fleets. The green areas pick out the regions that became known, as the men from Spain marched, rode, and sailed around the rich, sophisticated empire they found and crushed.

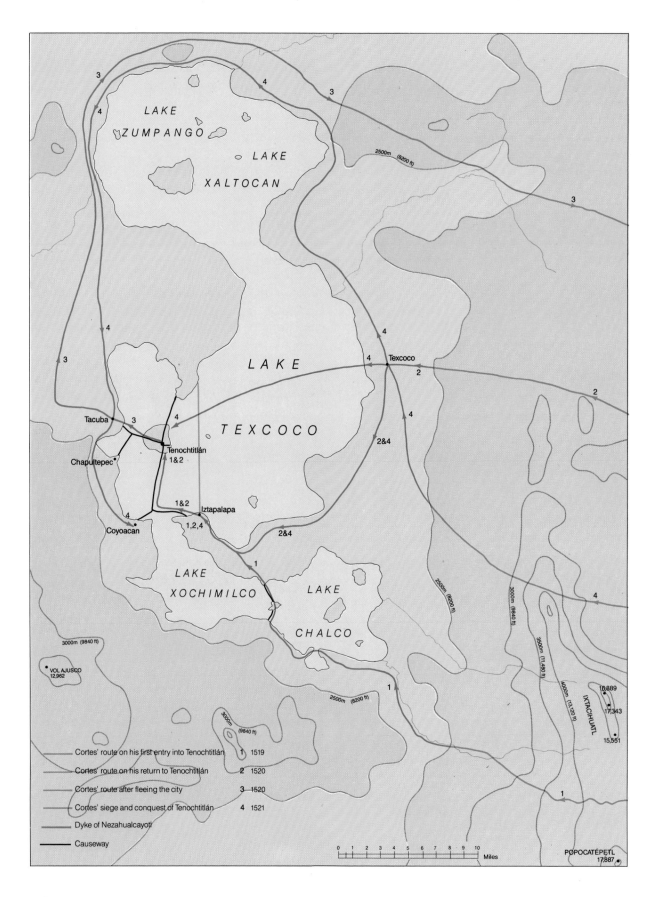

LAKE
ZUMPANGO

LAKE
XALTOCAN

2500m (8200 ft)

3

LAKE

TEXCOCO

4
Texcoco
2

4

4

2&4

Tacuba
3
4

Chapultepec

Tenochtitlán
1&2

1&2
Iztapalapa

1,2,4

2&4

Coyoacan
4

1

LAKE
XOCHIMILCO

LAKE
CHALCO

2500m (8200 ft)

3000m (9840 ft)

VOL AJUSCO
12,962

3000m
(9840 ft)

2500m (8200 ft)

2500m (8200 ft)

3000m (9840 ft)

3500m (11,480 ft)

4000m (13,120 ft)

IXTACCIHUATL

16,889

17,343

15,551

1

4

POPOCATÉPETL
17,887

	Cortés' route on his first entry into Tenochtitlán	1	1519
	Cortés' route on his return to Tenochtitlán	2	1520
	Cortés' route after fleeing the city	3	1520
	Cortés' siege and conquest of Tenochtitlán	4	1521
	Dyke of Nezahualcayotl		
	Causeway		

0 1 2 3 4 5 6 7 8 9 10
Miles

was thought to be an island and was given the name *Santa Cruz*.

Returning to Spain in 1528, Cortes was received with full honors by the king, and awarded the title of Marquess del Valle de Oaxaca. But his career was already on the wane. The king, fretful lest Cortes' powers and independence become too great, appointed an *audiencia* (a court of judges) to supersede his authority as governor. In 1535, Cortes' pride was damaged irreparably when he discovered that Antonio de Mendoza, the first Viceroy of New Spain, had the right to terminate the conquistador's office as captain general whenever he liked. Humiliated by these diminutions in his authority and the failure to establish a colony in California, Cortes sailed for Spain in 1540 to obtain redress for his grievances.

But this time the king turned a deaf ear to the former conquering hero. Spain had no more use for him. Many a subsequent conquistador, who had financed an expedition and taken all the risks to incur new possessions for the motherland, was to be accorded similar treatment. The effective power in overseas territories was invariably turned over to an intimate of the royal circle whose obedience to royal edicts could be relied upon without question. Attention was beginning to focus on the new territories in South America. Gold and treasure from Peru were fattening the Spanish treasury in amounts that eclipsed those derived from Cortes' New Spain. The most famous of all conquistadors was never to return to the scene of his many triumphs. One of his missives to his monarch reposed in government files for three years, unanswered. Written on the back were the words "no need to reply." Cortes died at the age of 63, embittered and broken in spirit.

Right: Indian laborers erecting a building under Spanish supervision. Mexico City, capital of New Spain, grew up on the ruins of the Aztec city of Tenochtitlán.

SEPTENTRIO

Terrade florid

Ocean'mocgñt

Noua galitñ

TROPICVS CANCRI

Mexico p.

Noua hispan

Sinus magnus Atliaru

Occanus occidens.

Mare de sul:

LINIA EQVINOCIALIS

Mare austrum:

Magnu mare occidetale.

TROPICVS CAPRICORNI

Mare. m. meridioms.

ORIENS

Nauicatio de magalhões.

Coronado and the Seven Cities

6

In March, 1536, a squad of Spanish cavalry was slave raiding in the region of the Sinaloa River, some 700 miles northwest of Mexico City. This distant outpost of New Spain, whose inhabitants were unused to Spanish ways, had been selected as a likely area for recruiting slave labor. But the Indians had taken to the hills, leaving the soldiers to chase one false trail after another. Suddenly, on the horizon, the troopers espied a group of stragglers ambling along at a leisurely pace. They galloped forward to make the capture. But on overtaking the unsuspecting victims, the Spanish soldiers halted in amazement. There were Indians certainly, 11 of them, but also a white man and a Negro. What were they doing in this out of the way place? Burned dark by the sun, and bone thin, the gaunt Spaniard, Álvar Núñez Cabeza de Vaca, looked more dead than alive. "They stood staring at me a length of time so confounded that they neither hailed me nor drew near to make an enquiry." Shortly after, he was joined by two more Spaniards in the same emaciated condition.

This dramatic encounter was the first news of an expedition that had set out from Florida eight years before, in 1528. The expedition under the command of Pánfilo de Narváez had long been presumed lost. But here, 2,000 miles from their starting point, were four survivors out of the original 300-man party. One was Cabeza, who had been the treasurer of the ill-fated expedition. Captain Alonzo del Castillo, and Captain Andres Dorantes and his servant, Estevanico, a Negro slave of Moroccan origin, made up the foursome. All the others had perished. These four had crossed one-half of the unexplored North American continent on foot. From Florida, on the Atlantic coast, all the way to Sonora, a Mexican province on the Gulf of California, they had made their way through swamps, sun-scorched plains, and mountain ranges peopled by Indian tribes.

Instead of curbing the Spaniards' curiosity about the land to the north, Cabeza's tale of misadventure had the reverse effect. Coming at the time it did, it focused attention on an area that seemed ripe for Spanish domination. Why should one or two preliminary disappointments halt these glorious adventures? No conquistador had any real doubt that to the north there were kingdoms as rich as Mexico.

One legend in particular, that of the *Seven Cities of Cibola,* had a strong hold on the Spanish mind. The legend told of seven fabulously rich cities somewhere to the north in what is now the

Below: portrait of Antonio de Mendoza, first Viceroy of New Spain. Anxious to establish Spanish domination in the New World and win greater treasures for his king, Mendoza sent Fray Marcos de Niza and later Francisco Vásquez de Coronado to explore the vast region to the north of Mexico.

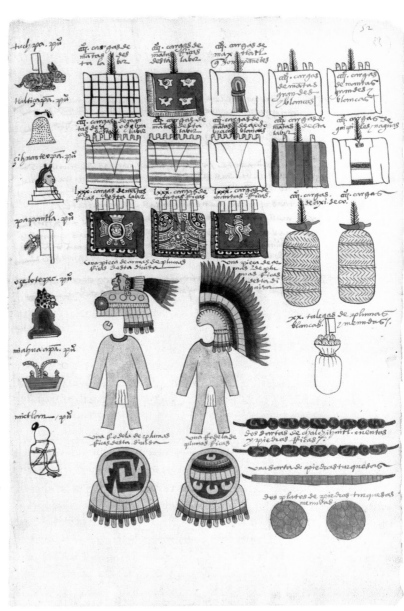

Above: an Aztec tribute list from the Codex Mendoza. The first column lists the Mexican towns that paid an annual tribute to the Aztec. The remaining illustrations show the types of tribute paid—among them cloth, warrior costumes, and cacao beans. Viceroy Mendoza commissioned the codex to explain Aztec culture to the Spanish court. (Bodleian Library, Oxford, MS. Arch. Selden A. 1. folio 52.)

Southwest United States. The Spanish imagination played havoc with fact. Knowledge of the continent north of New Spain was very sketchy. Only the Atlantic coast of North America had been mapped. The uncharted west coast was a mystery. And what lay inland? The question was compelling. Obviously the first man to come up with the answer to the riddle of the north would be rewarded by vast new possessions.

Antonio de Mendoza, Viceroy of New Spain, decided to send a small party into the north. Two candidates immediately sprang to mind. One was Fray Marcos de Niza, a Franciscan priest who had spent much time among the Indians in Hispaniola, Guatemala, Peru and Mexico. A second was the Negro, Estevanico, one of the four survivors of Cabeza's party, Estevanico's firsthand acquaintance with the religions and superstitions of the Indian tribes would be especially useful.

On March 7, 1539, with a small band of Pima Indians, the two hopefuls set off from San Miguel—which is in the Mexican state of Sinaloa. No more unlikely couple could have been chosen to lead the expedition. The two leaders almost parodied their differences. Fray Marcos, the soft-spoken priest, was dressed in plain, rough garb well-suited to his calling. The ebullient Estevanico, with his infectious grin and raucous laugh, had chosen a costume more suited for his role as magician and god. He sported plumes and feathers of brilliant hue, and to his arms and legs were attached little bells that tinkled with every movement he made. Remembering his days with Cabeza, Estevanico carried a magical gourd to which were attached red and white feathers. The gourd, when carried in advance by one of the Pima, was often accepted as a symbol of authority by the Indians.

As they progressed up the coast, the Indians they met instantly

Above: a Spanish friar baptizes a Mexican Indian. Large numbers of priests accompanied the conquistadors to the New World in order to convert the Indians to Christianity. Fray Marcos, one of the first white men to travel into what is now the Southwest United States, spent many years working among the Indians on the frontiers of New Spain.

recognized Estevanico as their long-lost friend and both he and Fray Marcos were eagerly welcomed as "Children of the Sun." Throngs of Indians clung to the small procession. The group was a welcome contrast to previous Spanish slave-raiding parties. Proceeding up the western coast of Mexico, they crossed the Yaqui River, and then turned inland through the lovely valley of the Sonora River. Here Fray Marcos halted his men in a small village. He then dispatched several Indians of his original retinue to survey the coast. While waiting for their return, Fray Marcos sent Estevanico ahead into the unexplored regions of the north as pathfinder. Fray Marcos stipulated that on no account was Estevanico to go farther ahead than 150 miles. The Negro was to send back reports via

Left: a page from the Codex Azcatitlan depicts the work of the Spanish friars as seen by their Mexican converts. Although the tonsured friar in his simple brown robe was a common sight in Mexico, the Indians of Arizona and New Mexico greeted Fray Marcos as a god.

Above: view of the Colorado Plateau—
a barren, broken country of deep canyons, sharp cliffs, and rugged, flat-
topped hills. Fray Marcos crossed parts
of the Colorado Plateau in his search
for the Seven Cities of Cibola.

his scouts as soon as he discovered anything of import. The size of
a cross would indicate the relative significance of the find. One the
size of a hand would indicate "but a mean thing found," twice the
size would show the discovery to be of some "great matter," and
"if more important than New Spain," a very large cross should be
sent.

After only four days, an Indian from Estevanico's escort appeared
bearing a cross the size of a man. The news was electrifying. The
Seven Cities of Cibola had been located! Not in his wildest hopes
had the friar expected such providential news so early in their
journey. Estevanico had found someone who had actually been to
the very metropolis hinted at by Cabeza. It was only 30 days distance to the north.

Estevanico had already set out for Cibola and by now had 300

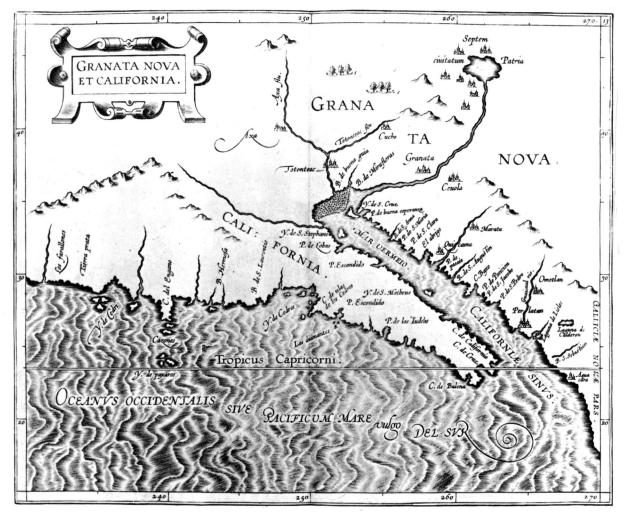

Map caption (top border): 240 250 260 270 · 13

GRANATA NOVA
ET CALIFORNIA.

GRANA
TA

NOVA

CALI-
FORNIA.

MAR VERMEIO

CALIFORNIÆ
SINVS.

GALLICE NOVÆ PARS

Tropicus Capricorni.

OCEANVS OCCIDENTALIS SIVE PACIFICUM MARE vulgo DEL SVR

Indians in his train. As soon as Indian scouts returned from the coast, Fray Marcos set out to meet Estevanico. The priest traveled north into present-day Arizona and then northeast into New Mexico, into the land of the Zuñi Indians. Here he ascended the high Colorado Plateau between the Rio Grande and Little Colorado River.

It was at this point, when he was but three days short of his destination, that he espied an Indian making haste in his direction. Something terribly wrong must have happened. The messenger "came in great fright, having his face and body all covered with sweat, and showing excessive sadness in his countenance." A calamity had fallen. Estevanico was dead. Surrounded by a wide circle of admirers Estevanico had reached the gates of Cibola. Just at the moment that was to be his greatest hour, Estevanico's magic had deserted him. The reception he received from the townspeople was openly hostile. He was detained in a large house on the outskirts of the city overnight. The next day, the puzzled man was told he could go. It was his death sentence. He walked straight into a merciless hail of arrows. Estevanico is assured of his place in history. He had traveled three fourths the width of the United States. At the

Above: the fabled Seven Cities of Cibola are seen in the top right-hand corner of this map of New Granada and the California Peninsula made in 1598.

Above right: the Taos Pueblo in present-day New Mexico is similar to the Zuñi village first seen by Estevanico. The terraced houses, made of boulders or adobe, were sometimes four or five stories high.

Right: this portrait of Francisco Vásquez de Coronado, although not historical, agrees with contemporary descriptions of the conquistador. Coronado was sent by Mendoza to find and conquer the Seven Cities of Cibola.

time of his death, no man had covered more ground of the unexplored regions of North America.

Fray Marcos resolved not to return to New Spain until he had seen Cibola, even if he should die in the attempt. With a handful of Pima, more frightened than loyal, the determined priest continued north. From a hilltop, Fray Marcos first glimpsed the legendary city framed against the backdrop of the Zuni Mountains. Across the shimmering plain, in the deceptively bright light of an altitude that magnified distant objects, he saw a collection of stone buildings, some rising higher than others. He judged the city to be larger than Mexico City. This was undoubtedly the Cibola of the legend. Dedicating the discovery to Saint Francis, he claimed possession of the land for Spain. This done, Fray Marcos hitched his skirts above his knees, and, in his own words, "with much more fear than victuals," sped for home.

The fair city that the priest had merely caught a glimpse of soon became in the telling the equal of Tenochtitlán. Fray Marcos did little to discourage such speculations. As for Mendoza, he already considered this new territory as won. The only decision left was to

Colorado

Grand Canyon
6C
Colorado
Plateau
Little Colorado
Tiguex 6
6 Cibola
Cicuye 6
Rio Grande
Arkansas
6?
6
6
6
Canadian
Brazos
Pecos
Gila
6A
6B 6B
6B
Sonora
Yaqui
6A
Sinaloa
Culiacán
Rio Grande
GULF OF CALIFORNIA
Lower California
TROPIC OF CANCER

3d
3d
3d
5
6A 6
3d
4
4
4
3b
4
M E X I C O
Pánuco
3b
2
BAY OF CAMPECHE
Tula (Tollan)
3a
3a
3b
3a
Tenochtitlán
3a
3c
Veracruz
2
2
Tabasco
3b
3d
4
5
3d
4
4
5
3d
Acapulco
5
4
4
5
5
4
4
5
5

GUL

M E

G U L F

PACIFIC   OCEAN

120°   110°   100°   90°

	Córdoba	1	1517
	Grijalva	2	1518
	Cortes (with Alvarado & Olid)	3a	1518–21
	Cortes	3b	1521–2
	Cortes	3c	1524–6
	Army (after departure of Cortes)	3C	1526
	Cortes	3d	1532–5
	Expeditions by Cortes' captains (Alvarado & Olid)	4	1521–41
	Maritime expeditions sent by Cortes	5	1522–39
	Coronado	6	1540–2
	Alarcón (with fleet)	6A	1540–1
	Diaz (in search of Alarcón)	6B	1540
	Cárdenas	6C	1540–1

0   100   200   300   400   500
Miles

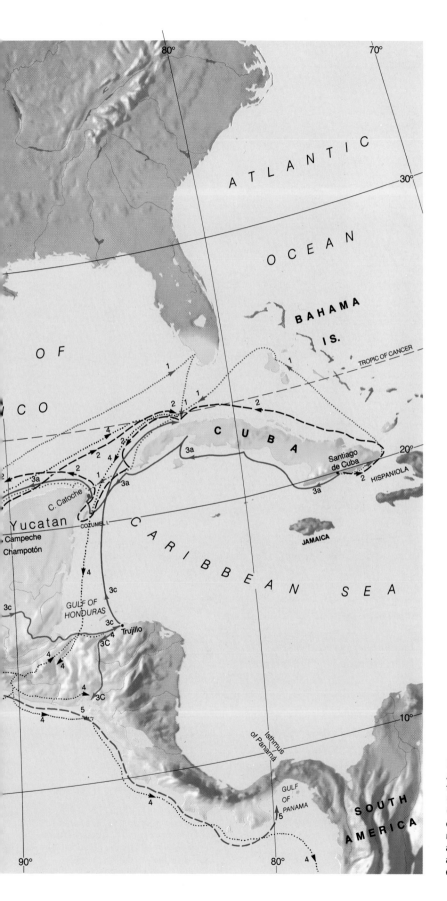

ATLANTIC

OCEAN

BAHAMA

IS.

OF

CO

TROPIC OF CANCER

1

1

2 1 1

2

C U B A

4

2

2

4

3a

20°

2

2

2

4

Santiago
de Cuba

3a

1

C. Catoche

3a

2 HISPANIOLA

COZUMEL I.

3a

Yucatan

Campeche
Champotón

C A R I B B E A N

JAMAICA

4

3c

S E A

3c

GULF OF
HONDURAS

3c

3c

4 Trujillo

3C

4

4

4

3C

4

5

Isthmus of Panamá

10°

4

GULF
OF
PANAMÁ

SOUTH

5

4

AMERICA

90°

80°

4

Left: this map of Mexico and Central
America shows the routes traveled by
the early Spanish explorers, from
Córdoba and Cortes in the 1510's to
Coronado in the early 1540's. The
conquistadors pushed north into what is
now the American Southwest, and south
along the Pacific coast of the Americas,
all the time hoping to find another Indian
empire as rich and rewarding as the Aztec.

appoint a commander to lead an expedition of conquest. He bestowed this honor on his young friend Francisco Vásquez de Coronado, the 29-year-old governor of New Galicia, the northwest province of New Spain.

On February 23, 1540, Coronado set out from New Galicia with 300 young men newly arrived from Spain. Many were of the aristocracy. Their blue blood, however, did not prevent them from being, as one observer noted, "for the most part vicious young gentlemen who did not have anything to do." They were accompanied by Indians, some Negroes, and 1,000 horses. Two ships under the command of Hernando de Alarcón conveyed the heavy equipment and stores on a parallel course up the west coast of Mexico. Alarcón was also instructed to survey the Pacific coast, and meet Coronado on an uncharted river.

Above: Coronado leads his men across the deserts of New Mexico and Arizona in search of the legendary Cibola. Although he found no civilization comparable to that of the Aztec, Coronado explored much of the American Southwest before returning to New Spain.

Right: a New Mexican Zuñi Indian practices the craftsmanship of his ancestors. The handsome turquoise and silver jewelry made by the present-day Zuñi is similar to that first seen and described by the conquistadors.

Advancing up the coastal strip, Coronado's large army made only sluggish progress. They spent three comfortable weeks at Culiacán. Frustrated at the slow pace of the cavalcade, Coronado decided to lead a flying column and make straight for Cibola. On April 22, 1540, he set out with his most trusted captains at the head of a small party of soldiers. Fray Marcos was also in the party.

The vanguard proceeded up the Sonora Valley and over the mountains into southern Arizona. Continuing north they crossed miles of parched deserts and rugged mountain ranges before reaching the high Colorado Plateau. Cibola lay just over the New Mexico border.

The ever-watchful Zuñi signaled their approach to Cibola by smoke signals. In July, 1540, they reached the Indian city. Coronado gazed eagerly across the plain and saw at once that it was nothing like the "silver city" that Fray Marcos had described. It resembled, rather, a collection of huts of varying height, all jumbled haphazardly together. The sight was a bitter blow to all. They had been on the march for the best part of five months and had covered 1,500 miles of torturous country. They had been in constant danger from hostile Indians and starvation. They had been promised glory, honor, and riches at the end of their journey. The humble Zuñi pueblo before them fulfilled none of their hopes.

The disappointed Coronado requested permission to enter the city peaceably. When this overture was rebuffed, the *requerimento* was delivered in all solemnity. When the Zuñi realized that they were being asked to give up their settlement without a fight, they were angry and bewildered. What sort of fools did the strangers take them for? They began to taunt the outnumbered Spaniards, thinking that they were too afraid to fight.

Coronado had no alternative but to attack. His men had not eaten for days and would starve unless they obtained provisions from the town. It took the conquistadors less than one hour to seize Cibola. But the Zuñi put up a fierce and bitter defense. "For myself," wrote Coronado, "they knocked me down to the ground twice with countless great stones which they threw down from above, and if I had not been protected by the very good headpiece which I wore, I think that the outcome would have been bad for me."

It was time to break the dismal tidings to Mendoza. "It now re-mains for me," wrote Coronado, "to tell about this city and kingdom

Above: "The Battle of Pueblo Oa-Quima," painted by Jan Mostaert about 1545. The picture is probably based on Coronado's report to the Spanish king on his expedition in search of Cibola. The landscape is pure fantasy. The Spanish soldiers, seen advancing from the right, are met by naked Indians trying to defend their strange clifftop dwellings. The animals in the foreground are reminiscent of a typical European pastoral scene of the same period.

and province of which [Fray Marcos] gave your Lordship an account. In brief, I can assure you that in reality he has not told the truth in a single thing that he said, but everything is the reverse of what he said, except the name of the city and the large stone houses. For, although they are not decorated with turquoises, nor made of lime nor of good bricks, nevertheless they are very good houses. . . ."

Coronado's attempts to open negotiations with the vanquished Zuñi were successful. The Indians came out of hiding from a neighboring pueblo. They were made to understand the Spaniard's request

to meet with their "prince" or "ruler" although the Zuñi had no
history of being governed by princes or kings. "They do not have
chiefs as in New Spain," observed one of Coronado's officers, "but
are ruled by a council of the oldest men. They have priests who preach
to them, whom they call 'papas'. These are the elders. They go up on
the highest roof of the village and preach to the village from there,
like public criers, in the morning while the sun is rising, the whole
village being silent and sitting in the galleries to listen. They tell
them how they are to live, and I believe that they give certain com-

Above: an imaginary portrayal of Coronado's search for the kingdom of Quivira. The Indian, El Turco, is seen on foot, pointing toward the east. During their fruitless search for Quivira, the Spaniards traveled through what is today the state of Kansas.

mandments for them to keep, for there is no drunkenness among them . . . nor sacrifices, neither do they eat human flesh nor steal, but they are usually at work."

The Indians of the adobe pueblos had plenty to eat, the land belonged to everyone, and what they built, they built to last. Unlike the majority of Indian tribes on the North American continent, the Zuñi were not nomads. They were a sedentary people with fixed traditions and a strong sense of duty to family and community. They worked hard for their stability but they had no understanding of the value of material things in the European sense. To them, a turquoise was valuable because of its sparkle and luminosity. There was no marketplace set up to determine its value. Why put a price on a thing of beauty?

The Spaniards, on the other hand, had come looking for gold and treasure and they were bitterly disappointed when they found there was none. Their disappointment soon turned to anger and in their fury they cared little for the finer points of the Zuñi culture—a culture that appeared backward and heathenistic to them.

By this time, the main body of the army had not yet arrived at Cibola, and still there was no word of the ships commanded by Alarcón. Coronado sent Melchior Diaz to see if he could locate the

vessels. Fray Marcos, whose life was threatened by the angry soldiers, took this opportunity to slip away from Cibola.

Diaz accompanied Fray Marcos as far south as the Sonora Valley. Then taking 25 Spaniards and some Indians, he headed northwest. Near the mouth of the Colorado River, Diaz found letters from Alarcón buried near the foot of a tree. Alarcón had sailed north along the coast of Mexico as far as was possible. He had confirmed beyond a doubt that so-called "Santa Cruz" was not an island but a peninsula, later known as Lower California. There, where the Colorado River empties into the Gulf of California, Alarcón had waited for news of the army. When no word came he decided to move farther north.

Crossing the treacherous shallows, Alarcón took some small boats and proceeded up the Colorado River. It is thought he reached a point beyond the Gila tributary, in which case he could be said to be the true discoverer of California. But the farther inland he penetrated, the more desolate the surroundings became. One moment there was nothing but barren stretches of desert, the next they would be going "between certain very high mountains, through which this river passes with a narrow channel." It was from the Indians that he had heard of Coronado's exploits in Cibola.

Above: the 1,450-mile-long Colorado River, one of the major waterways in the United States. The river takes its name from the Spanish word *colorado* meaning "colored red," because it flows through canyons of red stone. It was first explored by Alarcón in 1540.

Left: drawing of an American buffalo from a contemporary account of Coronado's expedition. Coronado was one of the first white men to encounter the American "crooked back oxen," and was quick to recognize its importance to the American Indian, who looked to it for food, clothing, and shelter.
Below: Coronado and his men on the banks of the Arkansas River. After penetrating the American Great Plains, Coronado abandoned his search for riches and returned to New Spain.

Alarcón returned to New Spain without achieving a link-up with the land forces. Nevertheless, he had accomplished a great deal. He was the first to map the Gulf of California with any accuracy, and the first to explore and describe the Colorado River, the mightiest waterway in the southwest United States. It was not until 300 years later that anyone would equal his efforts in the area.

Meanwhile, at Cibola, high on the Zuñi Plateau, Coronado dispatched search parties to see if a more attractive province could be located. Captain Pedro de Tovar went northwest and after 100 miles came across the Hopi Indian pueblo of Awatapi in northeast Arizona. The inhabitants refused to surrender. After bitter fighting the Indians were defeated. There was no gold.

About the same time that Alarcón had reached his farthest point up the Colorado River, García López de Cárdenas, another of Coronado's officers, was following its course from the opposite direction. Neither was destined to meet, due to the virtually impassable natural obstacles. Cárdenas and his men were the first white men to gaze upon one of the seven natural wonders of the world. Crossing the Colorado Plateau, they were suddenly confronted by that immense rent in the earth's crust that is now known as the Grand Canyon. The conquistador had met his match. After three days attempting a descent, Cárdenas knew it was unconquerable.

Coronado and the main body of the army waited at Cibola for news of some rich territory, the conquest of which might justify their expedition. One day, a young Indian chief with an extraordinary long mustache, strode into Coronado's quarters. After presenting him with some handsome gifts, the chief offered to lead a Spanish party to his pueblo in the east where the inhabitants, he promised, would look upon them as friends. The Spaniards were quick to nickname the agreeable young man "Whiskers." Coronado ordered Hernando de Alvarado to proceed at once to Whiskers' pueblo of Cicuye situated by the Pecos River.

Alvarado's small band traveled 80 miles to the east before coming

ALFRED RUSSELL

across a pueblo of any size. Then they headed northeast. As they neared present-day Bernalillo, in New Mexico, the desolate land changed to one of fertile, green pastures. The Spaniards called the area *Tiguex*. Here, a cluster of 12 pueblos, sheltered on the east by the Sandia Mountains, and watered by the upper reaches of the Rio Grande River, offered a refreshing contrast to the lands they had been journeying through. It was September and winter was fast approaching. Because Cibola was too small and remote to accommodate the entire army and its livestock, Alvarado sent a messenger to Coronado recommending that they set up their winter quarters at Tiguex.

Guided by Whiskers, the party continued on its northeast path. When they arrived at the chief's village, high up in the Santa Fe Mountains, they received a tumultuous welcome. While at Cicuye, Alvarado became acquainted with a man known as *El Turco* (The Turk). He was a servant of Whiskers, and a stray member of one of the Plains Indian tribes. El Turco told Alvarado that there was an abundance of gold in the kingdom of Quivira to the east. In Quivira, "there was a river in the level country which was two leagues [five miles] wide, in which there were fishes as big as horses, and very big canoes, with more than 20 rowers on a side, and that they carried sails, and that their lords sat on the poop under awnings, and on the prow they had a great golden eagle. . . . He said also that everyone had their ordinary dishes made of wrought plate, and the jugs and bowls were of gold."

With the wily El Turco in tow, Alvarado hurried his departure from Cicuye to bring this good news to Coronado. At Tiguex, where the army was now camped, El Turco told Coronado that when he was first captured by Whiskers he had stolen a gold bracelet he was wearing. If only he could lay his hands on the bracelet, he could show the Spaniards the quality of the gold in Quivira.

Eager for the sight of gold, the Spaniards returned to Cicuye to track down the ornament. Brushing aside the effusive welcomes, Alvarado demanded that Whiskers bring him the gold bracelet. Whiskers was perplexed by the sudden change in those he took to be his friends. He told Alvarado that there was no gold and that El Turco's story was a lie. But so intent were the conquistadors in believing in the wealthy kingdom of Quivira, that they preferred to take the word of El Turco. Alvarado arrested Whiskers and one of the oldest and most respected men of the pueblo. He took his captives back to Coronado at Tiguex. As one observer remarked, "This began the want of confidence in the word of the Spaniards whenever there was talk of peace from this time on."

On April 23, 1541, the Spanish army left Tiguex and headed directly for Cicuye, where they released Whiskers. The expedition then swung southeast from the Pecos to the Brazos River and made a loop due north across unending stretches of prairie where herds of wild buffalo grazed. In northeastern Texas, the Spaniards encountered the Tejas Indians from whom Texas derives its name. When Coronado asked them of Quivira, they could not corroborate El Turco's story.

It was now the end of May. Coronado had led his men over 600 miles of unexplored territory. The food supply had dwindled dangerously. He decided to lead a flying squadron to Quivira, due north, taking with him 30 horsemen, a few foot soldiers, and some Tejas as guides. The rest of the army were to stay where they were. Within a week Coronado promised to send back word whether they were to join him or return to Tiguex. When the orders came, the army was directed to make their way back to the winter camp.

Coronado's force pushed north into present-day Oklahoma. They crossed the Canadian River and continued to the Arkansas. They were now in Kansas, at a point just east of the future site of Dodge City. The general then wheeled the column in a northeasterly direction. Finally, having traveled 400 miles since leaving the main army, they came across El Turco's Quivira on the Kansas River. It was a modest Wichita Indian encampment where the inhabitants, terrified at the sudden arrival of the conquistadors and the strange animals on which they were mounted, cowered in their huts of grass and thatch. El Turco received instant justice. He was strangled.

Coronado took possession of this disappointing kingdom in the name of the Spanish king. He then led his men, dispirited and weary, back to Tiguex. The plan was to rest for yet another winter, then head north past Quivira in the spring of 1542. But an accident changed these plans. While taking part in a horse race, Coronado was thrown under the hoofs of an oncoming steed. The horse trampled over the leader who at one point was thought to be on the verge of death. Coronado recovered slowly, but, weary of the northern plains, he feigned illness in order to cut short the abortive expedition.

Leaving nothing but hate, fear, and violence in its wake, the Spanish army returned to New Spain. Many soldiers deserted as soon as they neared their homesteads. The bedraggled army was less than 100 strong when it drew up its ranks to face the displeasure of the viceroy at Mexico City. Mendoza had expected much more from the young Coronado. Cárdenas wrote, "Coronado came to kiss the hand of the viceroy and did not receive so good a reception as he would have liked, for he found him very sad . . . because this was the outcome of something about which he had felt so sure."

Coronado can hardly be blamed for failing to find something that

Below: Spanish friars are slain by embittered Indians. Because Coronado's forces had conquered many Indian villages, they left behind them a legacy of misery, suffering, and hatred. The result was the torture and death of the few Spanish friars who chose to remain with their new converts.

was not there in the first place. His achievements were considerable. He had blazed a trail across the Southwest United States, from Mexico to Kansas. His men had discovered the Grand Canyon and explored the Colorado River. He had reported competently on the customs and habits of the various Pueblo communities. Nevertheless, for Mendoza's purpose, he had come back empty-handed. The whole expedition had been a fiasco. The northern continent had become anathema to the gold-hungry conquistador and no one was to make a move in that direction for another 40 years.

Explorers, Conquerors, and Colonizers

7

Above: portrait of Francisco Pizarro, the conqueror of Peru. Pizarro was almost 50 years of age when he set out with a handful of men to topple the largest empire in the New World.

Left: Pizarro's dress sword, with its velvet handle and delicate filigree, was acquired only after the conquest of Peru had made him a rich man. It probably bears little resemblance to the rough steel sword with which the impoverished adventurer drew his famous line and initiated the conquest of the Inca empire.

Taking his sword, Francisco Pizarro traced a line in the sand and straightened up to address his men. "Friends and Comrades! on that side are toil, hunger, nakedness, the drenching storm, desertion, and death; on this side, ease and pleasure. There lies Peru with its riches; here, Panama and its poverty. Choose, each man, what best becomes a brave Castilian. For my part, I go to the south." This said, he stepped over the line. On that day, in 1526, on the island of Gallo off the coast of Colombia, 13 Spaniards elected to stand by the side of their leader.

The man with whom the 13 valiant soldiers had irrevocably linked their fate was an elderly man by the standards of the times. Francisco Pizarro was almost 50 years old. But his utter disregard for personal comfort while following a course of action with almost obsessive single-mindedness won him the respect and allegiance of both young and old. Before his death he was to conquer, without the aid of Indian allies, an empire stretching more than 2,500 miles down the South American continent.

Pizarro was born about the year 1478 in Trujillo, Spain. His birth was the result of what the Spaniards delicately refer to as a *desuedo* (negligence). His father was a retired army officer, Colonel Gonzalo Pizarro, and his mother a woman without rank. The colonel was to be "negligent" on at least two other occasions, the results being Gonzalo and Juan Pizarro. But he did have legitimate offspring, the proud Hernando Pizarro, who reckoned himself socially superior to his brothers.

In 1502, Francisco Pizarro went to the West Indies to make his fortune. He lived for some time on the island of Hispaniola (present-day Haiti and Dominican Republic) before joining the colony of Darien in what is now Panama. About the year 1520, Pizarro entered into a bizarre partnership with Diego de Almagro, an illiterate adventurer. Short and ugly, the middle-aged Almagro combined fantastic energy with a flair for business. He was likeable, generous, and light-hearted. The two adventurers were joined by a priest, Fernando de Luque. De Luque later earned the nickname *Fernando El Loco* (the crazy) for associating himself in what were thought to be hairbrained schemes. De Luque was on friendly terms with Panama's governor, Pedro Arias de Avila (Pedrarias), and possibly through his influence, the three prospered in their joint mining and farming ventures.

Long before this time, rumors of a vast southern kingdom on the western side of South America reached Panama. The first official government survey to the south of Panama had taken place in 1522 under the command of Pascual de Andagoya. Andagoya sailed south of the Gulf of San Miguel and reached the Biru River where he met Indian traders who told him of the rich and powerful Inca empire. It is thought that the name they gave the fabulous land was garbled by the Spaniards and came out as Peru.

Governor Pedrarias appointed a captain to search for the rich kingdom and, if possible, make contact with the Indian ruler. But the officer died without fulfilling his commission. Pizarro's group applied for and were granted the right to explore the area. Without delay the trio sold their estates and properties to raise capital for the enterprise. Pedrarias did not contribute a penny but declared himself in for an equal share.

In mid-November, 1524, Pizarro sailed from the newly established city of Panama near the country's Pacific coast. He was accompanied by 100 men. Almagro followed later in a second ship. Both men explored the Pacific coast of Colombia. They found tropical forests

Right: French map of part of Mexico, and Central and South America drawn in the year 1550. Less than 20 years after Pizarro landed in Peru, the coasts of South America were relatively fixed. Only the interior, with its mountains and mythical cities, remained a mystery.

Below: Francisco Pizarro, Diego de Almagro, and Fernando de Luque lay their plans for the conquest of Peru. The bizarre partnership between the two illiterate adventurers and the Catholic priest was to have a lasting effect on the history of South America.

MER D'ESPAIGNE;

MER OCCEANE;

DE CANCER:

MER DES ANTILLES;

LE PERV:

MER DV SV.

AMERIQVE

Amerique ou bresil.

la conqueste du perou faicte par les espaignolz

Canibales

LE PEROV.

MER DE MAGELLAN:

Riviere de plate PLATE

CAP DE FRIE:

estroict de magellan

103

Above: Pizarro's arrival on the Peruvian coast as depicted by a European artist in the 1500's. Crowds of hostile Indians are seen threatening the Spanish force.

and mangrove swamps housing hostile Indians but little gold. In the end they ran out of supplies and were forced to return to Panama. The expedition was a total financial loss.

Far from being dismayed at this setback, the ambitious trio immediately set about organizing another expedition. Gaspar de Espinosa, mayor of the city of Panama, agreed to finance this second undertaking. Pedrarias, convinced that the search was doomed to failure, was glad to sell his interest to Espinosa. With 2 vessels, 160 men, and 5 horses, Pizarro sailed from the Isthmus for the second time in 1526. This time he had been fortunate in securing the services of Bartolome Ruiz, who was a distinguished navigator. Ruiz immediately headed west out to sea and thus avoided the currents and the contrary southerly winds that had troubled and slowed the progress of the preceding journey. This time they landed in a more favored spot on the Colombian coast. Immediately inland they found settlements where richer samples of gold could be plundered.

Almagro was sent home with the treasure to gather more men and materials. Ruiz was to sail farther south to survey the coastal land.

Pizarro himself led a party inland in a frenzied search for gold and treasure. There was little to plunder and the old enemies—disease, hunger, and hostile Indians—took a steady toll in lives. But Pizarro's disappointment turned to elation when Ruiz returned.

Ruiz had sailed down the shoreline for several hundred miles to a point just below the equator. As he progressed farther south he had noticed increasing signs of civilization. There were towns, irrigated fields, people dressed in beautifully woven cotton garments, and substantial-looking houses of adobe brick. The high point of his survey had come when he encountered a large balsa raft quite far out to sea. The Indians aboard the raft wore beautifully made ornaments of gold and silver and were dressed in decorative garments of skillful weave. He had made the first contact with the Inca. Two of the Indians on board had told him of the Inca city of Tumbes, with its impressive buildings and its temple walls plated with gold.

This was the news Pizarro had been waiting for. When Almagro turned up with new recruits and stocks of provisions, the expedition resumed their exploration in high spirits. Ruiz' descriptions were accurate. They soon saw enough to know that they had stumbled

Above: this cross on the coast near Tumbes, Peru, marks the spot where Pizarro and his forces landed and began their march into the interior.

onto a kingdom worth exploiting, a second Mexico. But they were stalemated in proceeding farther. Despite the addition of new men they had not nearly enough troops to exploit these discoveries. At this stage, Almagro suggested he should return to Panama once more. With the impressive articles of gold and silver from their recent plundering, he would have no difficulty in raising an army of the size needed to bring the affair to a successful conclusion. Pizarro and Almagro nearly came to blows over this. Pizarro complained bitterly that it was always his lot to be left stranded in the most inclement

Above: map of the South American coast showing the island of Gallo. Pizarro and his men spent five months on the barren island awaiting supplies and reinforcements from Panama.

Left: mosaic ceiling and wall over Pizarro's tomb in Lima Cathedral. The artist portrays the conquistador's heroic stand on the island of Gallo, when, drawing a line, he chose to continue south to Peru rather than return to Panama. Thirteen soldiers decided to accompany their leader.

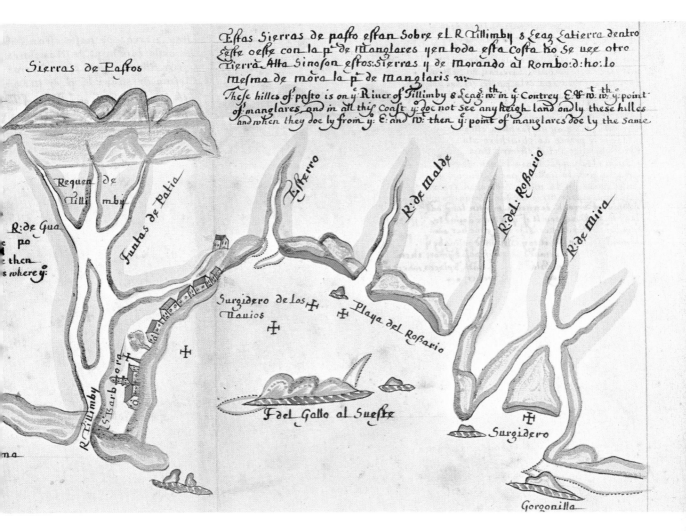

Sierras de Pastos

Estas Sierras de pasto estan Sobre el R Tillimby 8 Leag Latierra dentro
Leste oeste con la p de manglares yen toda esta costa ho se vee otro
Tierra Alta Sinoson estos Sierras y de morando al Rombo: d: ho: lo
mesmo de mora la p de manglaris m:——

These hilles of pasto is on y Riuer of Tillimby 8 Leag: w: in y Contrey E & w: w: y point
of manglares and in all this Coast y doe not see any heigh land only these hilles
and when they doe ly from y E: and w: then y point of manglares doe ly the Same

Requen de
Tillimby

Puntas de Patia

R: de Gua
po
e then
s where y:

El Ferro

R: de Malde

R: del Rossario

R: de Mira

Surgidero de los
Nauios

Playa del Rossario

S. Barbora

R Tillimby

I del Gallo al Sueste

Surgidero

Gorgonilla

surroundings, while Almagro returned to the colony in all comfort.
The argument was patched up for the time being and, when Almagro
left for Panama, Pizarro sent the other boat after him containing
some of the disaffected elements of his party. The old conquistador
and the remaining soldiers camped on the island of Gallo, off the
coast of Colombia.

When Almagro reached Panama, he found that Pedrarias had been
replaced by a new governor, Pedro de los Rios. De los Rios had no
interest in these excursions along the coast of South America. He
believed they were all doomed to failure and refused to take any
responsibility for the lives lost on the ventures. The governor dispatched two vessels to Gallo with orders to bring Pizarro and his
men home.

When the ships arrived at the island, Pizarro boldly refused to
return to Panama. It was at this time that he made his dramatic
appeal. Thirteen stalwarts defied the governor by standing firm
beside their chief. The ships sailed away, leaving Pizarro and his small
party stranded on the shores of Gallo. Almagro, however, managed
to prevail upon the governor not to abandon the tough old con-

Above: Pizarro at the Spanish court appealing for permission to conquer Peru. When the governor of Panama refused his consent for the venture, Pizarro sailed to Spain to appeal to the king personally. He carried with him gold and silver treasures he had looted on his earlier trips to Peru. The royal agreement was signed on July 26, 1529.

quistador. He argued that Pizarro and his men were only doing their duty for Spain and Saint James. The governor relented. He gave Almagro permission to join Pizarro insisting that they return within six months.

Pizarro, however, was to wait seven months before Almagro's sails hove into view. The party, at last reunited, proceeded southward. Sailing 250 miles below the equator they entered the Gulf of Guayaquil and landed at the city of Tumbes. When he went ashore, Pizarro saw large, well-constructed buildings. The busy populace went about their affairs dressed in fine apparel. It was by far the most civilized center he had seen since his arrival in the Americas over 20 years earlier. But it was the temple, sheathed in gold, that made the old warrior's heart leap with joy.

After sailing farther south, to what is now Santa, Peru, Pizarro returned home, eager to outfit an expedition. At Panama, they had been given up for lost. Instead of six months, Almagro had been away for 18 months. Unimpressed by Pizarro's treasures and stories of an Andean kingdom, De los Rios still refused to give his blessing to the enterprise. Faced with the governor's obstinate refusal,

Pizarro decided to go to Spain and appeal to the king himself.

Once Pizarro penetrated the royal circle his reception was unusually favorable. He paraded llamas and samples of gold and silver ornaments before the court, regaling it with stories of gold-plated temples. The conquistador convinced his sovereign that what had come about in New Spain could easily be repeated in Peru.

The royal agreement was signed on July 26, 1529. Pizarro was made governor and captain general of the lands he had yet to conquer. Almagro was appointed governor of Tumbes with less than half Pizarro's salary. Fernando de Luque was to be bishop of Tumbes and the faithful Ruiz was appointed grand pilot of the Southern Seas. Before his departure, Pizarro stopped at Trujillo and recruited his brothers—Hernando, Juan, and Gonzalo—and his half-brother Martin de Alcantara, to take part in the enterprise.

Pizarro's return from Spain was not an unqualified success. Almagro was furious at his downgrading. Hernando Pizarro treated the illiterate Almagro with a haughty attitude that did little to alleviate the troubled situation. But the differences were smoothed over. To placate the distrustful Almagro, Francisco Pizarro

Above: a silver llama, an alpaca, and the figure of a woman, all dating from pre-conquest Peru. These are among the few pieces of Inca metal workmanship that were not destroyed by the Spaniards. They are typical of the ornaments Pizarro carried with him to Spain and displayed before the Spanish court to impress the king and his ministers.

EL DECIMO CAPITAN CHALLCO CHIMA

Above: Peruvian warriors in battle, by an Indian artist. Pizarro arrived in Peru at the end of a civil war that had deeply divided the Inca empire and that was to facilitate the Spanish conquest.

promised that he would be amply rewarded after the conquest.

In January, 1531, Pizarro led his third and final expedition to Peru. His force consisted of 3 ships, 183 men, and 37 horses. Almagro, as usual, would follow later, but first he had the difficult task of enrolling recruits.

Pizarro's plan was to head straight for Tumbes in the Gulf of Guayaquil. But severe headwinds and storms forced them to put in at San Mateo Bay, 350 miles short of their objective. Impatient to begin his conquest, Pizarro disembarked his armor-clad troops and led them south through some of the worst terrain imaginable. The Spaniards attacked defenseless coastal settlements, gaining little, and assuredly losing any element of surprise. In the district of Coaque, however, they managed to loot a respectable haul of gold, silver, and emeralds. Pizarro's strategy now became clear. He sent back his ships to Panama, hoping that the sight of the treasure just won might act as an inducement for others to join. There was nothing for it but to advance to Tumbes by foot.

Left: the rival Inca emperors, Atahualpa (far left) and his brother Huáscar. The two sons of Huayna Capac waged a two-year civil war for control of the empire that their father had divided between them.

Since Pizarro's first visit to Tumbes, the city had been sacked and stripped of many of its treasures. At first the conquistadors were disappointed but when the reason for the state of affairs became known, the hopes of the whole party began to rise. A civil war had been raging throughout the Inca empire for the past few years. The Inca were now sharply divided into two camps. Pizarro immediately realized that the war-torn empire would be far easier to overcome than one united and strong.

At this point, Hernando de Soto (who would later explore the North American continent) arrived with much needed reinforcements. This enabled Pizarro to leave a garrison at Tumbes while he advanced 80 miles farther south to found the city of San Miguel, which afforded an excellent natural harbor at the mouth of the Chira River. There he learned from the Indians more details of the civil war. His timing could not have been better.

The war had been a struggle of succession between rival claimants for the Inca throne. The last emperor, Huayna Capac, had precip-

itated the crisis by dividing his kingdom between two sons. Atahualpa, his son by a Quito princess, was to govern the northern section of the Inca empire—what is today Ecuador. Huáscar, his legitimate heir (because he was the issue of his legal marriage with his sister), would rule over the rest of the mighty kingdom.

Huayna Capac died in 1527. An uneasy truce between the two brothers lasted for only a few years. Then a savage two-year war broke out. Pizarro had arrived at Tumbes shortly after Atahualpa's final crushing victory over his brother. Huáscar was in jail in Cuzco, and the usurper Atahualpa now considered himself ruler of the entire empire. He planned to make his triumphal entry into the capital but was unable to do so before news of Pizarro's arrival in Peru reached him. His camp both during and after the battle was at a sulfur spa high in the Andes. The name of the town was Cajamarca.

Above: the baths at Cajamarca, a sulfur spa high in the Andes. Atahualpa was encamped just outside Cajamarca after his final crushing defeat of Huáscar, when his couriers brought news of the Spanish landing in Peru.

Right: conquistadors on the march. Determined to capture Atahualpa in his mountain retreat, Pizarro urged his men on through the biting cold and rarefied air of the Andes. Strangely, the outnumbered Spaniards met little opposition along the way.

Cajamarca, 350 miles distant from where Pizarro and his men were assembled, could be reached in 12 days' hard marching. Cuzco, on the other hand, was 1,300 miles away and would take weeks to reach. When Pizarro learned that his quarry was camped in a relatively small town, and not the fortified capital of Cuzco, he was elated. He decided to act at once, without waiting for Almagro's reinforcements. With a force of 106 infantry, 62 cavalry, and a few cannon, Pizarro set out to conquer an empire.

In their heavy armor the conquistadors began a march of incredible difficulty. Leaving 80 men at the garrison in San Miguel, Pizarro led his soldiers southeast around the scorching Sechura Desert and then east, toward the ice-capped mountains. He proceeded toward the Andes in a steady but cautious manner, taking much longer than the estimated 12 days. Atahualpa had to be reached soon, but not at the price of weakening his men in rugged terrain.

Soon the Spaniards were ascending the Andes. It was the rainy season in the mountains and the party made perilous progress through the ravines. They advanced slowly along narrow paths over-hung by heavily barricaded fortresses. A handful of Inca warriors could have destroyed them at any time. The horses began to suffer from frostbite and the altitude made the men gasp for breath. Yet they met only scattered opposition. Apart from a few light skir-mishes there had been no hostility along the route. Had the civil war destroyed all effective opposition in these parts? Soon they were to find the answer. An Inca nobleman advanced on the party and bade Pizarro and his men welcome. Atahualpa would gladly receive the Spanish strangers as his guests at Cajamarca.

For some weeks now, Atahualpa had been watching the progress of the Spaniards with interest. He had no reason for fear. Whatever their intentions, hostile or otherwise, the Spanish soldiers were at his mercy. Atahualpa, secure after his great victory, could allow himself the luxury of waiting and seeing what happened before taking any precipitate action. His messengers had confirmed that their numbers were insignificant. Other reports indicated that their weapons were not particularly out of the ordinary. This would be a pleasant diversion before his journey to Cuzco.

Early in the evening of November 15, 1532, more than seven weeks after setting out from San Miguel, Pizarro and his men arrived at Cajamarca. The Inca encampment was spread out on the slopes

above. Pizarro found the town suspiciously quiet. No one came out to greet them. The leader cautiously led his men forward. When they reached the central plaza he sent his brother Hernando and Hernando de Soto to seek out the emperor. They were to invite Atahualpa to come "to meet his brother."

The Spaniards found the Inca ruler seated on a small stool attended by nobles and numerous officials. Francisco de Xeres, a Spanish soldier in the company of Pizarro records a description of the emperor's appearance: "Atahualpa was a man of 30 years of age, good-looking, somewhat stout, with a fine face, handsome and fierce, the eyes bloodshot. He spoke with much dignity, like a great lord. He talked with good arguments and reasoned well, and when the Spaniards understood what he said they knew him to be a wise man. He was cheerful; but, when he spoke to his subjects, he was very haughty, and showed no sign of pleasure."

At first, Atahualpa did not reply to the visitors' request. Only when Hernando Pizarro repeated his invitation in the politest of terms, did the emperor speak. He informed them that he was observing a fast that did not end until the following day. When his fast was over he would dine with the Spaniards. Hernando de Soto, an excellent horseman, chose this moment to impress the Indian ruler and his entourage. Wheeling his horse, he galloped at full

Left: a European engraving of De Soto's and Hernando Pizarro's meeting with Atahualpa. During the interview, the flamboyant De Soto wheeled his stallion at the Inca emperor. The Inca nobles, who had never seen a horse before, recoiled in terror. Only the emperor remained impassive.

Right: a drawing by the Inca artist Guaman Poma of the same scene. An Indian account of the incident states that De Soto's horse brushed so close to the emperor that he "felt the breath of the beast on his face."

Above: Atahualpa, advancing on a golden litter to meet Pizarro, is accompanied by his household and court. Nobles swept the road of pebbles and straw as the unarmed emperor and his court entered into Cajamarca.

speed toward Atahualpa, stopping so close to the seated monarch that the horse's nostrils almost brushed the Indian's face. Atahualpa, who had never seen a horse before, sat impassive and dignified. His attendants—not supported by royal dignity—had involuntarily shrunk back in horror. Some say that those who had shown fear were executed for displaying cowardice in front of the strangers.

The two captains returned to their leader, disappointed that the Inca, unlike the Aztec, had no superstitious dread of the foreigners. According to their calculations, there were 30 or 40 thousand warriors encamped on the hill. The Spaniards slept lightly that night.

At noon on the following day, Atahualpa advanced slowly toward the town. He was carried by his nobles on a golden litter. Attendants swept the ground over which he was to pass. The emperor had accepted Pizarro's invitation and had let it be known that he and his men were coming as guests, bearing no arms.

Pizarro was almost beside himself with joy at this last news.

La conquista del Peru.
llamadalanueua Castilla. La ql tierra po: diuina ro
luntad fue marauillosamente conquistada en la felicis
sima ventura del Emperador y Rey nuestro señor:y
pozla prudencia y essuerço del muy magnifico y vale
roso cauallero el Capitan Francisco piçarro Gouerna
dor y adelantado de la nueua castilla:y de su herma
no Hernando piçarro:y de sus animosos capitanes
z fieles y esforçados compañeros.q cõ el se hallaron

Left: Atahualpa is met, not by Pizarro, but by a Spanish friar with a bible and crucifix. Annoyed at the friar's impudence, Atahualpa threw the book to the ground. At a signal from Pizarro, Spanish soldiers, concealed in the city, rushed the royal procession. The soldiers put all to the sword, brutally massacring the Inca nobles who tried to protect their emperor.

Atahualpa was playing into his hands more easily than he had imagined possible. And having no doubt as to whose side God was on, the Inca's intimation that neither he nor his men would carry weapons seemed a divine answer to his prayers. He briefed his soldiers on a variation of the Montezuma kidnap. On the prearranged signal, the Spaniards concealed in the buildings surrounding the square were to open fire and then rush the imperial entourage. Twenty soldiers were detailed to seize the emperor and see that he came to no harm. The remainder were to be wiped out.

Atahualpa made his way into the square with his attendants numbering between three and four thousand. His entrance into Cajamarca had been strangely similar to Pizarro's on the previous day. The procession wended its way through the empty streets to the plaza in an eerie silence. There was no sign of the Spanish force. "Where are the bearded ones?" asked the Inca ruler. But it was a friar named Valderve, not Pizarro, who came forward to greet the

Inca emperor. Valderve carried a bible and crucifix and immediately began a long discourse on the Christian faith. He demanded that Atahualpa declare his allegiance to the Catholic Church and the King of Spain. Annoyed at the impudence of this lowly man who was insisting that he renounce his own divinity in favor of a crucified god, Atahualpa is said to have tossed the bible to the ground and with a proud gesture toward the sun to have exclaimed "My god still lives." At that moment Pizarro gave the signal. Soldiers and cavalry charged the unarmed Inca, slashing their way through the bodies. The massacre was over in 30 minutes. Atahualpa was Pizarro's prisoner. His bodyguard was dead or scattered. One of those who took part in the battle later commented: "As the Indians were unarmed they were defeated without danger to any Christian." The royal procession bedecked with gold, jewels, and feathers now lay dead, an inextricable tangle of blood-spattered bodies.

Atahualpa, under Spanish guard, continued to hold his court in miniature. In a desperate bid for freedom, Atahualpa made a fantastic offer to Pizarro. He promised to cover the floor of the room in which they were standing, an area 22 feet long by 17 feet wide, with gold. Pizarro, probably stupefied, did not reply at once. The Inca immediately raised his ransom bid saying that he would fill the room with gold and silver as high as he could reach (about seven feet) and he would do this in two months! Pizarro drew a red line marking the height. From that moment, streams of porters from all over the empire began piling one golden masterpiece on top of another.

In February, 1533, when Almagro arrived at Cajamarca with much needed reinforcements, Atahualpa had spent three months in captivity. The Inca emperor had fulfilled his side of the bargain. The room was filled with a golden treasure estimated as worth anything between $8 and $20 million. Now the thorny question remained— what to do with the royal charge? Honor demanded that Atahualpa be released on fulfilling his part of the bargain. Pizarro, however, recognized the strength of the man. Set at large the proud chief was capable of rallying his empire and wiping out the Spaniards.

Rumors began to multiply that the Inca army was massing in the south to attack the Spanish camp. Atahualpa denied that any such movement was in operation, but the Spaniards became increasingly nervous. They implored their leader to kill the emperor and thus end the threat of rebellion. Hernando de Soto along with a few others protested against such a flagrantly dishonorable solution.

As the months passed, the strain began to tell. The Spaniards, who had the riches of a lifetime, were in the paradoxical position of not being able to take advantage of their changed circumstances. Because supplies of iron were short, horseshoes were cast of silver. A piece of armor or a gun was worth a fortune in gold. The officers and men made fresh remonstrations to Pizarro to execute Atahualpa as a way out of all their troubles. Pizarro at first demurred, or for the sake of appearances, pretended to do so. Then he agreed to a trial.

The ruler of the Inca was accused of "treason," of trying to raise

Above: in a desperate bid for freedom, Atahualpa promised to fill a room seven feet high with gold and silver. Magnificent objects, such as this golden toucan (a common bird in Peru) were brought from all over the empire.

Above: the dark line marking the height
of the treasure can still be seen in the
ransom room at Cajamarca. The size of
the ransom was unparalleled in history.
Most of the best of Peru's artifacts
were brought here, melted down by the
Spaniards, and shipped to Spain.

Left: Indian messengers bring fine gold
ornaments, stripped from temples and
palaces throughout the Inca empire, to
fulfill Atahualpa's ransom promise.

Above: the trial and death of Atahualpa, by an unknown artist of the Cuzco school. After fulfilling his promise and amassing a fortune in gold for the Spaniards, Atahualpa was tried on trumped up charges, sentenced to death, and murdered by the Spaniards.

forces to overcome the Spaniards. However much Atahualpa denied this, he faced other accusations such as incest (the marriage with his sister), usurpation of the Inca throne, and just about anything else the Spaniards could think of. The court was assembled in August 1533. Prudently, Pizarro had sent De Soto with a small force to investigate a false rumor of troops congregating some distance from the town. When they returned to the camp, the deed was already done. Atahualpa had been found guilty and sentenced to death by fire. Just before the execution, his sentence was commuted from burning at the stake like a heretic, to strangulation. The judicial murder of the man who had kept his side of the bargain and who had given no intimation that he would ever have harmed the

Spaniards, was a simple measure of brutal expediency rather than justice.

Pizarro now resolved to move on the capital. Resistance was minimal. The Inca seemed completely demoralized by the swift turn of events. On November 15, 1533, just one year after his arrival at Cajamarca, Pizarro entered Cuzco with a force of 480 Spaniards. The restraint that the soldiers were forced to exercise on the march was abandoned as soon as they reached the capital. The beautiful city of Cuzco, over 300 years old, was stripped bare of everything of pos-

sible value. Temples, palaces, and homes were plundered. In some buildings, the Spaniards found planks of silver 20 feet long. Even the sacred mummies of earlier Inca emperors were looted of their jewels.

The Spaniards helped themselves liberally to everything. The Inca's ingrained obedience to whichever hierarchy was in power was mistaken for cowardice on their part. The inhabitants were tortured and raped at will. Their engineering marvels, such as the irrigation canals that had rendered wastelands into fertile havens, were allowed to fall into decay. The fields became fallow and llamas were killed off at such a rate that the breed was threatened with extinction.

When the rape of Cuzco was complete, Pizarro set about establishing order in the chaotic city. He appointed a new Inca emperor,

Above: Pizarro marched into Cuzco in November of 1533. The inhabitants were tortured, raped, and put to the sword, while the city itself was systematically stripped of everything of value.

CARIBBEAN SEA

80°

70°

60°

50°

ATLANTIC

OCEAN

—10°

Isthmus of Panama

Panamá

2a

2a

2c

1

2a

2b

2a

2a

2c

2b

Magdalena

6a

6a

6A

6a

6a

6a

6a

6b

Santa Fé de Bogotá

4

6b

Orinoco

6b

6b

Orinoco

8

8

3

3

GALLO

2b

2b

SAN MATEO BAY

2c

4

Quito

Cocoa

EQUATOR

EQUATOR

0°

0°

2c

Coaque

7

7

8

2b

7

Napo

7

2c

3

8

8

Tumbes

2b

7

4

A

San Miguel

2c

Amazon

Sechura Desert

N

2c

3

Cajamarca

2c

D

2b

7

E

—10°

—10°

2c

S

2c

3

2c

Lima

2c

9

9

7

2c

Cusco

9

5

A

5

5

L. Titicaca

N

9

D

9

E

5

PACIFIC

9

5

5

S

9

Atacama Desert

Tupiza

—20°

—20°

OCEAN

TROPIC OF CAPRICORN

5

5

5

....	Andagoya	1	1522
————	Pizarro, F. (followed by Almagro)	2a	1524–5
	Pizarro, F. (with Almagro & Ruíz)	2b	1526–8
	Pizarro, F. (with his 3 brothers & half-brother & followed by Almagro)	2c	1531–5
– – – –	Alvarado	3	1533–5
– – – –	Benalcazaar	4	1534
·········	Almagro	5	1535–7
··········	Jiménez de Quesada	6a	1536–7
	Supply ships	6A	1536
	Jiménez de Quesada	6b	1569–71
– – – –	Pizarro, G. (with Orellana)	7	1540–3
– – – –	Orellana	8	1541–3
————	Valdivia	9	1540–7

Copiapó

9

5

5

5

0   100 200 300 400 500

Miles

La Serena

from Valparaíso

9

9

to Santiago

—30°

Above: this equestrian statue of Francisco Pizarro, the conqueror of Peru, stands in the plaza at Trujillo, Spain, the conquistador's birthplace.

Left: this map of northern South America shows the routes of Francisco Pizarro, Almagro, Valdivia, and the other Spanish conquistadors as they explored the rugged western side of the vast continent. It also shows Orellana's amazing journey eastward down the Amazon to the Atlantic Ocean in 1541–1542.

Manco Capac II, as puppet ruler. Real authority, however, was vested in a town council consisting of eight *regidors*, two of whom were his brothers Juan and Gonzalo. Every Spaniard was allotted a house, a grant of land, and Indian servants.

Cuzco, located high in the Andes, was too far inland to serve as the center of Spanish trade with the mother country. Leaving his brothers in command at the ancient Inca capital, Pizarro traveled to the coast where he founded the new *City of the Kings* on January 18, 1535. The future Lima, located near the mouth of the Rimac River, was to serve as the headquarters of the Spanish government in Peru for the next 300 years. With characteristic vigor Pizarro exchanged his sword for the tools of an artisan and began the planning and construction of his capital.

Everything was quiet. The victory was complete. Or was it? Little undercurrents began to ripple the smooth surface of everyday life. These were not discernible to the new masters of the Inca empire. But they soon would be. The peace was illusory.

Below : Spanish soldiers ill-treating
their Indian slaves. After the conquest of
Peru, the Indian population was reduced
to slavery by the introduction of
the brutal encomienda system, the basis
of the Spanish colonial empire.

The Quest for an Empire

8

By 1535, the conquest of Peru was complete. This should have been the end of the epic adventure. But the spirit of the conquistador was a restless one and his appetite for gold was not easily satisfied. The vast South American continent held promises of still richer kingdoms for those who were willing to look for them. Thus began a period of exploration, during which the conquistador was to reach into the most inaccessible corners of the Andes Mountains and the almost impenetrable growth of the Amazon jungle. The conquistadors found no kingdoms equal to those of the Aztec and the Inca, but in the course of their search, they opened up the whole of South America.

Diego de Almagro was the first to look beyond the lands of the Inca. In reward for his part in the conquest of Peru, Almagro was appointed *adelantado* of the region stretching 500 miles below the southern extremity of Pizarro's lands. After an abortive attempt to claim Cuzco as part of his grant, Almagro began preparations to explore the lands farther south.

In July of 1535, accompanied by 570 Spaniards and several thousand Indians, Almagro left Cuzco. Herds of llama and swine, which were to provide food during the outward-bound journey, trailed behind the column of marching men. The first leg of the trip, along the Inca highway, was made quickly and with relative ease.

But 150 miles southeast of Cuzco, the Inca military road winds out of the highland valleys and ascends the Bolivian *altiplano,* a high, wind-swept plateau that is bordered on two sides by parallel ice-capped ranges of the towering *Cordillera* of the Andes. Almagro led his men along the western shore of Lake Titicaca—the world's highest inhabited lakeland area that today forms part of the border between Peru and Bolivia. The Spaniards were astonished to see the remains of elaborate stone buildings and huge megalithic structures whose precision-measured blocks weighed sometimes 100 tons. Here and there on the bleak altiplano stood tall columns with decorative friezes. The ruins were the last remnants of the Tiahuanaco civilization, which had flourished in the area from the A.D. 300's to the 900's. In the 1400's, the Inca had extended their rule throughout the plateau and, in consequence, Tiahuanaco architecture had profoundly influenced subsequent Inca construction.

As the Spaniards trudged along the barren altiplano, about 12,500

feet above sea level, they suffered severely. The soldiers struggled for breath and were blinded by the dazzling light of the rarefied atmosphere. As they made their way south through what is now Bolivia, food and water became scarce. Most of all they complained of the excruciating cold. It was midwinter and the treeless steppe offered no protection to an army on the march. Augustin de Zarate, a Spanish historian of the 1500's, states: "No clothes or armor were sufficient to keep out the icy wind which pierced and froze them." Men and horses began to drop out, undergoing agonies of frostbite from which many never recovered. "The ground was so cold, too, that when Don Diego [Almagro] returned to Cuzco 5 months later he found in various places men who had died on the way out frozen hard to the rocks with the horses they were leading; and their bodies were as fresh from corruption as if they had only just died."

At Tupiza, in southwest Bolivia, they reached the southern limit of the altiplano. The depleted force made its descent into the

Left: Inca reed boats on Lake Titicaca, the world's highest navigable inland lake. Almagro and his men marched along the shores of Lake Titicaca on their way south to Chile. Near the lake they encountered traces of the ancient Tiahuanaco civilization (A.D. 300–900). Below: early Spanish woodcut of Lake Titicaca. The artist has pictured an imaginary European city on its shores.

Left: Almagro and his forces crossing the Chilean Andes. Although the Spaniards suffered from the bitter cold and thin air of the Andes peaks, it was the Indian porters who underwent the greatest hardship. Unaccustomed to the extreme cold, unprotected by warm clothing, and struggling under their heavy burdens, more than 1,600 Indians died during the crossing.

Above: the "Peruvian sheep" or llamas as depicted in Zarate's *History of the Discovery and Conquest of Peru.* The llama was to prove invaluable to all Spanish explorers in South America.

secluded valley of Salta, in northwest Argentina. There they rested for the remaining winter months before resuming their march. The most difficult part of the journey lay ahead. The conquistadors now had to cross the towering peaks of the Andes that separate Chile from eastern South America. The casualties increased sharply as Almagro led his men through freezing mountain passes to Copiapó, in northern Chile. More than 1,600 men, mostly Indians, died during the march.

One of the stoutest members of the expedition was the llama, the animal peculiar to the Andes, which the conquistadors referred to as "Peruvian sheep." Zarate's account of the expedition gives a detailed description of the llama. "In all these wild places where there was no snow there was a great shortage of water, which the Spaniards carried in sheepskins, each living sheep carrying the skin of a dead

Above: the Pacific coast where Almagro and his men rested before continuing south. The mild, subtropical climate offered a welcome respite after the freezing cold of the Bolivian altiplano and the Andes Mountains.

one on its back filled with water. One of the characteristics of these Peruvian sheep is that they can carry a load of 50 or 60 pounds, like camels, which they much resemble in build though they have no hump. The Spaniards have since used them as horses, for they can carry a man 4 or 5 leagues [10 or 13 miles] in a day. When they are tired and lie on the ground, they will not get up even if beaten or pulled; the only thing to do is to take off their load. If they grow tired when ridden and the rider urges them on, they will turn their heads and spatter him with a very evil smelling liquid which they seem to carry in their crops . . . these animals are of great use and profit, for they have very fine wool, especially the kind that they call alpaca, which have long fleeces. They require little food, especially those that work; they eat maize and can go for three or four days without drink. Their flesh is . . . clean and succulent."

From Copiapó Almagro led his men south through a subtropical belt of the Chilean coastal strip. The soft breezes and abundant vegetation made a refreshing contrast to the savage cold they had endured on the barren Bolivian altiplano and the freezing Andean Cordillera.

Almagro halted the army near what is now Santiago in central Chile. By a circuitous route he had covered a distance of about 2,500 miles since leaving Cuzco. Nowhere had he seen a kingdom to rival that of the Inca. Because of the barrenness of the soil and the lack of easy treasure, Almagro was merely perfunctory in claiming title to the region in the name of the Spanish king. He was certain by this time that he would not settle in the lands in which he had been appointed *adelantado*. He determined to return to Peru and demand from Pizarro his proper share in the fruits of a venture in which they had set out as equal partners.

Before heading north, however, Almagro sent a reconnaissance party farther south in the hope that some rich kingdom might yet be discovered. The scouting party went as far south as the Maule River—the southern boundary of the former Inca empire. They encountered only savage and hostile Indians. There was little gold to be found. Although the land was green and fertile they preferred to tell their leader that it was drab and uninteresting and not worth pursuing. The soldiers were as anxious to return home as was their commander. The journey had been hard and the returns negligible. When news was brought that an Indian uprising had sparked a countrywide revolt in Peru, and that the Spaniards were in imminent danger of losing everything they had so recently won, Almagro hastened his departure north.

Profiting from the bitter lesson of the outward journey, Almagro resolved to avoid the peril and discomfort of the highland route by keeping as close to the coast as possible. The first stage of the journey, as far as Copiapó, was over familiar ground and was covered briskly and in comparative comfort. The soldiers were pleased to be going home.

Advancing north of Copiapó, the Spaniards found themselves on the threshold of the Atacama Desert, one of the most forbidding regions in the world. As they struggled forward, the sun beat down mercilessly with temperatures of over 100°F. No vegetation relieved the monotonous brown landscape. Hovering in the background,

Left: Inca warriors under Manco Capac II rebel against Spanish rule. On receiving news of the Inca uprising in Peru, Almagro hastened back to Cuzco.

Below: from their stronghold on a mountain peak, Indian warriors hurl stones and uprooted trees at the Spanish soldiers approaching below. The Inca, familiar with the terrain, were better equipped for mountain warfare than the Spaniards who were encumbered by their horses and heavy armor.

El Adelantado Don Diego de Almagro. Capitan General

+ El Marq. Don Francisco Pizarro de Puerta

Franco Pizarro y sus compañeros estan en la ysla Gorgona

Franco Pizarro Sale de Panama a descubrir

Franco Pizarro de la Puña pasa a Tumbez

Los Castellanos llegan A la Baya de san Mateo

HISTORIA GENERAL DE LOS HECHOS DE LOS CASTELLANOS EN LAS ISLAS Y TIERRA FIRME DEL MAR OCEANO Escrita por Antonio de Herrera Coronista Mayor de SU MAGESTAD de las Yndias y Coronista de Castilla y Leon DECADA QUARTA AL REY Nuestro Señor

Los de Tumbez debaxo de seguro dan en los Castellanos

Los Castellanos pasan a la Isla Puña

Edifica el primer templo en S. Miguel de piura y Herdo de Soto pelea con los yn

los Castellanos pelean con los Indios en la puña

El Adelantado Don Pedro de Alvarado de Badajoz

la Batalla de Vtlatlanga dio don Pedro de Alvarado a los yndios

Diego de Ordas Reconoce el Volcan de Tlaxcala

+ El Capitan Diego de Leon

Left: page from Herrera's *General History*. In the top left-hand corner is the conquistador Diego de Almagro, on the right Francisco Pizarro. Other drawings show incidents from their conquest of Peru. At one time close friends, Almagro and Pizarro fell out over the division of their spoils. Their quarrel resulted in a civil war among the invading Spaniards that lasted for 11 years.

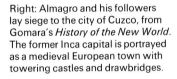

Right: Almagro and his followers lay siege to the city of Cuzco, from Gomara's *History of the New World*. The former Inca capital is portrayed as a medieval European town with towering castles and drawbridges.

the ice-capped western Cordillera of the Andes seemed to mock the soldiers as they trudged through the blistering heat of their present route.

In April of 1537, Almagro's force reached the outskirts of Cuzco. There they learned that Manco Capac II, the puppet-ruler, had escaped and rallied the Inca nation to rise up against the Spaniards. Hernando and Gonzalo Pizarro, with 200 Spanish soldiers, had been besieged in their mountain camp at Cuzco since February 1537, some 19 months after Almagro had left for Chile. Francisco Pizarro was at Lima on the coast and was powerless to help the beleaguered fortress. His own force was relatively small in numbers, and the lines of communication between Lima and Cuzco had been cut by Manco Capac's forces.

The Inca were far more experienced in mountain warfare than were the Spaniards. As they darted from their clifftop fortresses and laid their ambushes in narrow mountain passes, the Indians attacked with relative impunity. Encumbered by their heavy armor, breathless from the high altitude, and separated from supplies and reinforcements by miles of mountainous territory, the Spaniards were no match for the Inca warriors. Augustin de Zarate described the Inca's successful tactics. "The Indians let the Spaniards enter a very deep and narrow valley, and blocked both the entrance and the way out with great numbers of men. Then they hurled so many stones and boulders down on them from the slopes that they killed almost all of them without coming to close quarters; and from the dead, who amounted to more than three hundred, they took great quantities of jewels and arms and silk clothing."

Foolishly, the Inca allowed themselves to be drawn into open battle by Almagro and his men. The battle took place in a valley near Cuzco and the Inca were soundly defeated. It was a decisive turning point in the conflict. From that time on, organized resistance to the Spaniards petered out into sporadic raids from mountaintop fortresses such as Vilcapampa and Machu Picchu. Almagro entered Cuzco both as liberator and conqueror. He chose this moment to make good his previous claim to the city.

The Inca were now treated to the spectacle of a civil war between their conquerors, as the followers of Pizarro fought the Almagro faction for supremacy. On April 26, 1538, Almagro's forces were defeated on the plain of Las Salinas near Cuzco. The aging conquistador was brought before Hernando Pizarro for trial. Almagro begged for mercy: "I was the first ladder by which you and your brother mounted up. When I held you as you now hold me and all counselled your death, I alone gave you life." Hernando rebuked Almagro saying that these were no fit words for a man of courage and that he should prepare to meet his death "like a Christian and a gentleman." "I am human and may fear death, since Christ himself feared it," was the reply. The old adventurer, who had played a large part in the conquest of Peru and had explored hundreds of miles of unknown territory, was summarily tried and executed in July, 1538.

Almagro's death was only the first step in a power struggle that was to last for 11 years. Three years later, on June 26, 1541, Almagro's death was avenged when a band of his followers murdered Francisco Pizarro in his palace at Lima. The conquistador's death is described by Augustin de Zarate: "They all fell on the Marquis with such fury that he was too exhausted to brandish his sword. And so they finished him off with a thrust through the throat. As he fell, he cried for a confessor. But his breath failed him. Making a cross on the floor, he kissed it and so gave up the ghost." "Thus one sees,"

Right: capture and death of the conquistador Diego de Almagro. Defeated by Hernando Pizarro at the Battle of Las Salinas, Almagro was tried and executed in July of 1538.

Below: Francisco Pizarro is murdered at the palace in Lima. Although the conquistador was killed by Almagro's followers three years after their leader's death, the Indian artist has depicted Almagro himself thrusting his sword through Pizarro's heart.

Zarate continues, "the way of the world and the varieties of fortune: that in so short a time a gentleman who had discovered and governed great lands and kingdoms . . . should be killed . . . yet none of them came to his aid."

While the power struggle between the supporters of Pizarro and the followers of Almagro raged in Peru, the search for new sources of gold and glory continued. Rumors of mysterious kingdoms in the interior of present-day Colombia and Venezuela flourished. The most haunting of the legends that grew up was that of the *El Dorado*—a mythical South American king who supposedly powdered his body with gold dust each morning and washed it off every evening in a lake. The name El Dorado also referred to a fictitious kingdom located somewhere on the Amazon. During the search for the kingdom of El Dorado, northwest South America was opened up.

In April of 1536, Gonzalo Jiménez de Quesada set out to explore the forbidding interior of Colombia. He traveled overland through the swamps and jungles of the coastal region and finally reached the Magdalena, Colombia's chief river. Penetrating farther inland, Quesada came upon hints of a superior civilization. He was nearing the kingdom of the Chibcha Indians who lived on the high plains of the central Colombian Andes. The Chibcha were an advancing civilization with temples, statues, and a currency system. In time the Chibcha civilization might have rivaled those of the Maya, Aztec, and Inca. They worked gold, drilled emeralds, made pottery and basketry, and wove textiles. Theirs was the last civilization of any great wealth to be found in South America.

Politically divided, the Chibcha fell easily to Quesada's forces, and the valuable Colombian highlands, rich in minerals and emeralds, was incorporated into Spain's empire in the New World. On August 6, 1538, Quesada founded the town of *Santa Fé de Bogotá*, which became the capital of the Spanish Viceroyalty (province) of New Granada (present-day Panama, Colombia, Ecuador, and Venezuela). Today, Bogotá is the capital of Colombia.

The discovery of the kingdom of the Chibchas focused attention on the northern segment of South America. No expense was spared as one expedition followed another in an effort to capture the glittering prize of El Dorado. Wily Indians fired the conquistadors' insatiable desire by luring the strangers in the one direction left

Right: title page from Book VI of Herrera's *History*, depicting several incidents from the civil war that raged between the followers of Almagro and Pizarro. The page includes a portrait of Gonzalo Jiménez de Quesada in the upper right-hand corner. Quesada explored the interior of Colombia while searching for the legendary city of El Dorado. He conquered the Chibcha Indians and founded the city of Bogotá in 1538.

El Mariscal Alonso de Alvarado

El Licenciado Gonzalo Ximenes de Quesada descubrio el Nuevo Reyno de Granada

Batalla de Benalcazar

Prision de Atahualpa Rey del Piru

Almagro y Alvarado se conciertan

HISTORIA GENERAL
DE LOS HECHOS
DE LOS CASTELLANOS
EN LAS ISLAS Y TIERRA FIRME
DEL MAR OCEANO
Escrita por Antonio de Herrera
Coronista
Mayor de SU MAGESTAD
de las Yndias y Coronista de Castilla
y Leon
DECADA SESTA
AL REY   Nuestro Señor

Batalla de Abancay

El Mariscal Rodrigo Organes

Sitio del Cuzco

Adelantado Sebastian de Benalcazar

Batalla de las Salinas

unexplored. To the east of Peru lay an enormous basin drained by
the chief river of South America—the 4,080-mile-long Amazon. The
impenetrable jungle stretching the length of the river was rumored
to hold not only the fabulous kingdom of gold, but large tracts of
cinnamon trees.

In 1540, Gonzalo Pizarro set out from Cuzco to find the riches that
had so far eluded everyone. Early the next year, accompanied by a
large cavalcade of soldiers and Indians, and soon to be met by
Francisco de Orellana, Pizarro left Quito in a blaze of triumph. The

Left: the Amazon River winds sinuously through the jungles of Brazil. The longest river in South America, the Amazon takes its name from the legendary female warriors said to have been seen by Francisco de Orellana, the first white man to navigate the river to its mouth.

expedition crossed the eastern Cordillera of the Andes and descended into the dense jungle growth of the Amazon basin. In order to make their way through the solid blanket of green, the Spaniards were forced to cut a path with their swords. In November 1541, they reached the banks of the Coca River, which flows into the Napo, one of the tributaries of the Amazon. When they reached a point where the river became navigable, Pizarro ordered the construction of a small boat to carry the sick and the heavy supplies. The march along the swampy river bank continued. Food became scarce and the men were forced

Above: Pedro de Valdivia, conqueror and second governor of Chile. The young conquistador was appointed by Francisco Pizarro to found a colony to the south of Peru. Valdivia led his expedition to Chile in 1540.

to live off wild roots and nuts. Hostile, primitive Indians sporadically attacked the weary men.

Near the junction of the Coca and Napo rivers, Pizarro halted the army and sent Orellana ahead in the boat to forage for food. It was Christmas when Orellana set out with about 50 men and most of the supplies and weapons. He made rapid progress downstream. The small craft, swept onward by a strong current, passed the junction of the Coca and Napo, and raced on toward the Amazon. Finally, having covered 500 miles in 8 days, Orellana landed at a small village where there was a supply of food. The problem now was how to carry the food back to Pizarro. The current was so strong as to make an upstream voyage virtually impossible. Abandoning Pizarro and his men to their fate, Orellana continued to the mouth of the Amazon, thus becoming the first white man to explore the full course of South America's longest river.

Pizarro and his men waited in vain for Orellana's return. Desperate with hunger and exhaustion, the men "leaned against the trees and begged for food, but [they were] so thin and weak that they died of starvation." Deprived of his boat, and without adequate weapons or supplies, Pizarro was forced to fight his way back through the difficult terrain he had just covered. Finally, the tattered remnants of the once hopeful expedition reached the vicinity of Quito. A Spanish commentator described the pitiful condition of Pizarro and his men as they neared the city. "They were traveling almost naked, for their clothes had rotted long ago with the continuous rains. . . . Their swords were sheathless and eaten with rust. They were all on foot, and their arms and legs were scarred with wounds from the thorns and bushes. They were so pale and disfigured that they were scarcely recognizable."

While Gonzalo Pizarro was planning his ill-fated search for the kingdom of El Dorado, a smaller expedition set out quietly from Peru. Led by Pedro de Valdivia, this expedition to the south excited none of the enthusiasm or support that characterized Gonzalo's venture. Valdivia had been commissioned to found a colony in Chile. Because of Almagro's report that Chile held no treasure and that the routes south were of indescribable difficulty, Valdivia had a difficult task recruiting men for his expedition. "All fled from it as from the plague and many sane men thought I was insane." By January, 1540, however, he had accumulated sufficient numbers to

Mare antilarum. SEPTENTRIO

Peru. Mare aquedulcis EQVINOCTIALIS

America

Lambales. Brasilis.

Quarta orbis pars.

TROPICVS CAPRICORNI

Terra argetea.

Mundus nouus.

Terra Incognita

ORIENS

Mare inuentu p magalhões.

Above: Spanish laborers construct a building in Santiago, the city founded by Pedro de Valdivia in 1541.
Below: an early prospect and plan of the settlement of Santiago.

make a start. The expedition consisted of 150 Spaniards, 1,000 Indians, and horses and swine.

Profiting from Almagro's experience, Valdivia led his men south along the Peruvian coastal strip and across the Atacama Desert into Chile. The Indians, angry at this new invasion by the Spaniards, concealed foodstuffs from the passing convoy, making the trek even more difficult for Valdivia and his men. It was several months before the exhausted Spanish force reached Copiapó—the first habitable settlement after the barren wastes of desert lands.

Continuing south for another 400 miles, the Spaniards found themselves in a beautiful, fertile valley at the foot of the Andes Mountains. There, in February, 1541, Valdivia traced out the plans for a city. The streets, main plaza, and sites for the town hall, church, and prison were in the grand Spanish style. He allotted each Spaniard a *repartimiento* of land and Indian laborers. As wooden huts with thatched roofs sprang up in the beautiful green turf, Valdivia's settlement took root. Such was the humble beginning of Santiago, the capital of modern Chile.

Due to his extraordinary powers of leadership, Valdivia was able to avert one crisis after another that plagued the colony in its early years. The land itself was isolated from Peru. Not only distance but the natural physical barriers of desert and mountain cut off Chile from the rest of South America. The unusual ferocity of the Indians frustrated early attempts on Valdivia's part to develop the resources of the colony. The Spaniards themselves were by no means united in their desire to live and work peacefully in the fertile valley. Many had come solely to find another Mexico or Peru and to win immediate riches. They took the first opportunity to complain at the land grants allocated to them by Valdivia and demanded huge numbers of Indians to work for them. Dissension among the colonists rose to mutinous levels.

Three months after the establishment of Santiago, Valdivia received rumors of Pizarro's assassination. It had become known that the friends of Almagro were conspiring against Pizarro. The legitimacy of Valdivia's grant was called into question by the unexpected events in Peru. The newly constituted town council of Santiago decided to settle the issue in its own way. It nominated Valdivia as governor and captain general of Chile, pending ratification by the Spanish king. Valdivia eventually made it clear that he would

Right: despite fierce opposition from the Araucanian Indians, the city of Santiago flourished. By the 1800's, it had become one of the most important centers of trade in South America.

Below: today Santiago is the capital and largest industrial city in Chile. Replacing earlier colonial buildings, skyscrapers now rise in the shadow of the snow-capped Chilean Andes.

accept nomination for the governorship but would recognize only those representatives legally appointed by Spain.

Anxious to keep informed of events in Peru, Valdivia decided to establish a sea link with the northern country. He led a detachment of men to a harbor site, 60 miles from Santiago, that he had noticed on his journey south. There, just north of modern Valparaíso, he ordered that a ship be constructed. A sea route would be infinitely preferable and faster than the overland alternatives. While on the coast a plot to overthrow the leader and seize control of the Chile expedition was revealed in Santiago. Valdivia quelled the rebellion by returning at once to the capital and executing the ringleaders.

No sooner had he returned to Santiago to cope with the dissident elements within his own ranks, than Valdivia was confronted with the news that the small garrison he had left at the coast had been wiped out by the Indians. Only two survivors had escaped the massacre. The Indians, encouraged by the success of their first strike against the white intruders, concentrated all their efforts on driving the Spaniards out of the land completely. Waiting until Valdivia and the main body of the army were engaged outside the town, they attacked Santiago in full force. The 50 Spaniards trapped inside the fort were heroic in its defense and the Indians were put to flight. But by the time Valdivia and the army had returned, the town had been reduced to rubble and smoldering embers. "Not one post standing: we had nothing but our arms and the old rags which we wore in the fight."

There was nothing to do but to start rebuilding the city from scratch. The conquistadors became farmers and construction workers as the settlers engaged in a desperate attempt to keep the colony alive. Help was sought from Peru, and a party of six men, carrying as much gold as could be mustered, was dispatched north to secure supplies and reinforcements. Three of the party were killed by Indians at Copiapó but the remaining three men eventually reached Lima. They arrived in Peru just after Vaca de Castro, the new governor from Spain, had defeated the Almagrist army.

The desperate force at Santiago were compelled to wait two years before relief came. In September, 1543, a ship arrived in Valparaíso bringing food, supplies, and a relief force of eight men. From that time forward, ships and men began to dribble into the isolated colony.

Above: present-day Valparaiso, Chile's main port and fishing center. Lying 60 miles west of Santiago, Valparaiso was founded by one of Almagro's officers in 1536.

Left: an early map of Valparaiso. The port was a vital link in Chile's communications with the rest of Spain's colonies in South America.

Gradually, Valdivia began to broaden his sphere of operations. To the north, in the Coquimbo Valley, Valdivia built a town in 1545, and named it La Serena after his birthplace in Spain. A reconnaissance party to the south reported that the area was ideal for settlement. The land was fresh and green, suitable for both farming and grazing.

But before Valdivia could establish settlements in the south, he was called back to Peru to aid in putting down yet another rebellion. In 1544, Gonzalo Pizarro had challenged the legitimate viceroy's authority by declaring himself governor of Peru. Valdivia defeated

Pizarro's forces at Sacsahuamán—the Inca fortress at Cuzco. The President of the *Audiencia* of Lima rewarded him by confirming his title to Chile and extending the area of his governorship.

Valdivia returned to Chile in the early part of 1549, arriving in the aftermath of a serious revolt in the northern part of his domain. The uprising was severely put down and for the next few years all was comparative peace and quiet. Fields of corn and wheat flourished and the livestock multiplied. Chile was becoming a land of plenty. Valdivia established more towns to the south of Santiago, where the

Above: an Araucanian family in their traditional dress. The Araucanians in southern Chile successfully resisted Spanish domination for 300 years. They finally signed a peace treaty with the Chilean government in 1883.

Right: the Araucanians took horses from the Spaniards in the mid-1500's and moved freely between Argentina and Chile, fighting the Spaniards on the coast and fleeing to the mountains for refuge. Secure in their mountain retreats, the Araucanians found time for sport and recreation. Here, a group of Araucanian boys are seen playing a form of hockey.

146

green fertile land was watered by crystal clear streams and shaded by large forests. Concepción, which was soon to rival Santiago in importance and size, was founded in 1550.

But the period of grace for the Spaniards was running out. The Araucanian Indians of southern Chile particularly resented the presence of the strangers. Their resistance continued for 300 years. The Araucanians were a proud, fierce, and warlike tribe who refused to be enslaved by the white men. The atrocities of the Spaniards (400 Indian prisoners were mutilated by cutting off their right hands

and noses) infuriated the Indians who closed ranks against the oppressors. Their knowledge of the impenetrable forests and other peculiarities of the terrain gave them an advantage over their foe.

In December, 1553, while riding in the region of Concepción, Valdivia came across a Spanish fort that had been raided by the Indians. Accompanied by only a small force, he determined to seek out the perpetrators of the deed at once. The Araucanians were waiting for him.

Valdivia attacked, but the terrain was unfavorable for his horses and the attack was turned into an undignified retreat. It is said that Valdivia could have made good his escape but, when he saw his chaplain in difficulties, preferred to stay at his side. He was captured and tortured to death.

The Indians followed up their victory by storming Concepción and other southern towns. The inhabitants fled to Santiago. For three years, the Indians made devastating attacks, and reinforcements and supplies from Peru could barely keep up with the minimum supply needed to fight off the relentless strikes. Eventually, in April 1557, the Spaniards won a key victory and Chile was saved for Spanish domination. For the next 300 years, however, the Bío-Bío River in southern Chile remained the frontier of their dominion. The Araucanians were undisputed masters below this line. After a huge expenditure in lives and money had been wasted in attempting to subdue the belligerent tribe, the Spaniards left them to their own devices.

By 1550, most of South America had been conquered and explored by the Spanish conquistadors. Only Brazil, which Orellana had described as inhospitable and which legitimately belonged to Portugal, remained outside Spanish rule. In less than 25 years since Pizarro's first landing in Ecuador, Spain's coffers had been filled with a fortune in gold and treasure. More important, the basis of continued Spanish control had been firmly established in the form of settlements and towns scattered throughout the continent. In their quest for gold and glory, the conquistadors had won for Spain a vast and sprawling empire that was to last for almost 300 years.

Right: this statue of Pedro de Valdivia stands in Santiago's main square – the Plaza de Armada. Valdivia died at the hands of the Araucanians in 1553.

End of an Era

9

"Broken spears lie in the roads,
We have torn our hair in grief.
The houses are roofless now . . .
And the walls are red with blood. . . ."

(Elegy for Tenochtitlán)

Tenochtitlán is dead. Four hundred and fifty years ago the passing of the Mexican city was mourned by an unknown Aztec poet. He saw it razed to the ground before his eyes. We shall never see it, this city of palaces and pyramids, of raised causeways across the lakes, of stone statues and turquoise masks. We shall never view the royal processions of priests and kings ablaze with jewels and plumes. We shall never follow the colorful canoes laden with fruit and native Mexican flowers as they glide silently in the watery streets. The city of the Aztec is gone. Only the snowy peaks of the Sierra Madre Mountains remain impassive and unchanged by the Spanish intrusion.

A thousand years before Columbus arrived in the New World, the Mexican high tableland had witnessed the rise and fall of many civilizations. But when the Spaniards arrived, the greatest of all Mexican empires was in the making—a colossus stretching from the arid steppes of northern Mexico to the burning jungles of the southern isthmus. The city of Tenochtitlán was barely 200 years old when it fell to the echo of steel blades against swords of volcanic glass, guns against arrows and spear-throwers, iron helmets against feather headdresses.

How did the Spaniards, so greatly outnumbered and with such dangerously extended supply lines, uniformly win the battles of conquest? Part of the answer lies in their weapons and horses. The explosion of a gun terrorized the Indians, while men on horseback were at first taken to be single creatures, awesome in their power. Imaginative campaigning, as in Cortes' use of brigantines on the waters of the Valley of Mexico, contributed to particular campaigns. The Indians were weakened psychologically through their superstitious myths, that sometimes foretold defeat at the hands of white and bearded strangers coming from the east. The Spanish policy of alliances with rival Indian tribes often equalized or minimized the initial imbalance in numbers. Thus, Cortes profited from the long-established hostility of the Tlaxcalan toward the Aztec. And Pizarro could hardly have made his way so readily through the Inca

Above: the brutal reality of the Spanish conquest of the Americas is illustrated by this simple Inca drawing of a Spaniard ill-treating his Indian servant.

Right: Santiago (Saint James), patron saint of the conquistadors, from a painting by an unknown artist of the Cuzco school. The archetypal soldier-saint is pictured with upraised sword crushing his enemies beneath him. The battle-cry "Santiago!" rang out on every field of battle as the conquistadors fought their way to victory over the American Indians.

Above: Indian allies, hostile to their Aztec overlords, played an important part in the Spanish conquest of Mexico. In this Indian drawing, a Tlaxcalan warrior is seen pulling the armor-clad Cortes from a canal in Tenochtitlán.

empire without the civil war of succession that divided its people. Finally, Indian allies provided and transported goods, thus reducing the threat of overextended supply lines.

The confrontation between Aztec and Spaniard was more than just a meeting between two expanding nations—it was a clash between two radically different cultures. The Spaniards thought the Indian was an inferior species, a creature more animal than human, destined by God for slavery and serfdom. Moreover, he was guilty of tyranny, human sacrifice, cannibalism, idolatry, and other sins. The Aztec, on the other hand, thought the strangers represented Quetzalcoatl and other gods returning from over the sea. The Spaniards—despite their astonishment at the magnificent temples, palaces, and gardens of Tenochtitlán—considered the Aztec no better than barbarians.

The Europeans were not even sure that the Indians were human

Above: Indian laborers lay the cathedral foundation in Mexico City.
Below: a Spanish friar instructs the Mexicans in the Christian religion. The Church's interest in the Indians' spiritual welfare did not deter them from exploiting Indian labor in the building of churches and monasteries.

beings. Did they have immortal souls? Should they be baptized? These were not idle questions. For Columbus and the powerful Spanish nation that he served, the spreading of the Christian gospel was an integral part of national policy. The theologians soon decided that the Indians did in fact have immortal souls and were proper subjects for conversion. Unfortunately for the Indians, they wore gold ornaments and jewels. The Spaniards had set out not only to spread the gospel but also to trade in the spices of the East. The prospect of finding gold and jewels softened their disappointment at failing to find the spice routes. The slight regard the Indians had for the ornaments they wore seemed to prove conclusively that the land was full of riches.

As Spain's need for more and more gold to maintain its naval supremacy increased, the Spanish adventurers were required to send vast stores of wealth back to the mother country. They were their

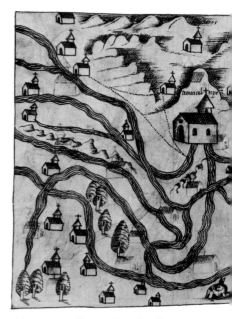

Above: an early map showing the profusion of churches that sprang up after the Spanish conquest. During the colonial period, about 12,000 churches were built in Mexico alone.

own judges of the methods they used to get them. To find these realms of gold, adventurers probed along the coast and up the rivers, led expeditions into the interior, and built bases from which to organize systematic searches. In their minds, gold and glory were always uppermost. They had not left Europe, as many North American colonists had, to escape war or persecution, nor did they propose to carve a new home from the virgin territory. But while seeking gold and glory they had to eat, and that meant that food had to be grown. Gradually, as the illusion of ready-made wealth faded, many cut their dreams down to size and adjusted to living off the land.

Nevertheless, they still refused to work with their hands. Instead, the conquistador—both nobleman and commoner—continued to make the Indians do the work. The Indians found it less convenient. They lacked the physical stamina for steady exertion. They died off like flies in the gold mines of Hispaniola, under brutal Spanish overseers. On the great estates, too, the Indians were victimized by cruel overseers.

To the burdens imposed by this lay aristocracy were added those of supporting the Church. Christianity was represented at first by government-paid friars, who accompanied every expedition. The holy fathers often won the affection of the Indians by protecting them from the cruelties of the conquistadors. But even the friars could be harsh in the interests of God. Pagan temples had to be replaced as rapidly as possible by Christian churches. Indian laborers were made to quarry the stones, while Indian craftsmen carved them and set them in position under Spanish supervision. Every valley in central and southern Mexico was dominated by the towers and domes of churches—12,000 were built in Mexico alone during the colonial period. The churches testified not only to the triumph of Christ over Huitzilopochtli, but to the skill of his missionaries in obtaining unpaid labor from the Indians.

The most disastrous result of the Spanish conquest, however, had little to do with the cruelty of the conquistadors. The Spaniards had brought with them European diseases—smallpox, measles, influenza—against which the Indians had no natural immunity. Smallpox was rampant even before the fall of Tenochtitlán. Another disease, which first appeared during the viceroyalty of Mendoza, killed the Indians by the hundreds of thousands and then swept

Right: La Antigua, the oldest church on the American mainland, was founded by Hernando Cortes at Veracruz shortly after the Spaniards' arrival in the New World.

Below: Indians suffering from smallpox, from a contemporary illustration. The Spaniards brought new diseases and infections with them to the New World. During the 1500's epidemics of smallpox, measles, and influenza swept through the Americas killing hundreds of thousands of Indians.

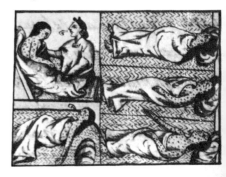

across New Spain again and again during the following 200 years. At the time, the disease was attributed to the influence of a comet or to volcanic fumes. It was, apparently, a strain of influenza. In turn, the Indians infected the Spaniards with syphilis—a kind of biological revenge. The result of these diseases was a heavy decrease in population. For hundreds of years, Mexico was never so thickly inhabited as before the Spanish conquest.

Spain, in contrast to the English colonies to the north, regretted the depopulation caused in Central and South America. The Spaniards—in spite of the practices that killed Indians by the tens of thousands—depended on them to exploit the riches of the conquered lands. In Spanish America, the Indians were regarded from the start as subjects of the Spanish king, and the authorities in Spain did their utmost to ensure that they should be protected, converted to Christianity, and instructed in useful crafts.

Bartolome de las Casas, the first monk to protest effectively

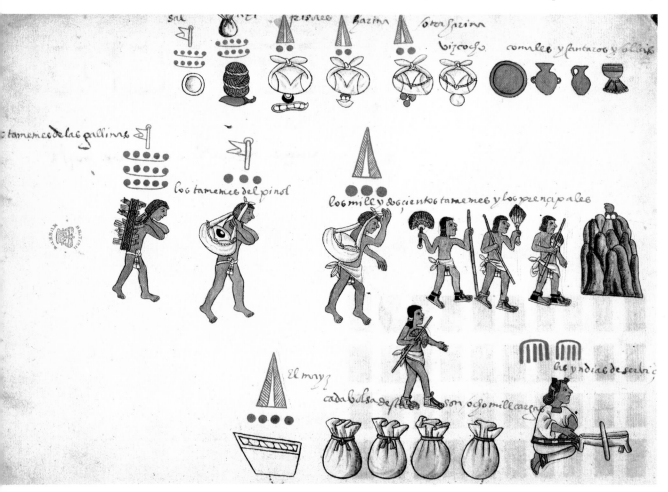

Above: Indian representation of the encomienda system from the Kingsborough Codex. Under the system, Indian labor was leased to the Spaniards who, in turn, were responsible for the physical and spiritual well-being of their charges. Not unnaturally, the system led to unjust exploitation of the Indians. Addressed to the Royal Audiencia, the Kingsborough Codex complained of the excessive duties imposed by Spanish overseers.

against Spanish cruelty, spent a long lifetime working among the American Indians. He and others had the legal status of the Indians spelled out. The basic institution created to protect them was the *encomienda* that introduced the European feudal relationship of lord and vassal. The Indians were to be brought together in villages where they would be under the authority of a Spaniard. They were not slaves but free men in the eyes of the law, entitled to certain rights in return for specified services.

The Spaniard undertook to "convert, civilize, and educate" the Indians in his service, while guaranteeing them possession of the lands owned by the village. In return, the Indians had to work in his fields or mines. In practice, there was nobody to see that the Spaniards carried out their part of the bargain. Despite the protests of Las Casas and other missionaries, the Spaniards gradually established rights over the village lands and reduced the Indians, in effect, to slaves. Large numbers, nevertheless, survived and were gradually incorporated into the Spanish culture, forming the basis of the modern population. The process of incorporation was facilitated by the intermarriage of Spanish men and Indian women.

The New World was conquered by conquistadors. But most of the men whose qualities had made such extraordinary achievements possible were not of the stuff of empire-builders. Even the role of explorer had been purely incidental. Their business was fighting. Success did not break them of the habit and most of them died violent deaths in the power struggles that followed upon each new conquest. Consolidation of the empire they gained was left to others.

The conquistadors and their lands were controlled by a bureaucracy whose members were sent out from Spain. At the top of the administrative pyramid was a viceroy who lived in royal magnificence and

Above: this painting of the 1700's shows the double wedding of two Inca ladies and two Spaniards. The woman on the left is robed in the traditional Inca ceremonial dress, while the bride on the right wears European costume. Intermarriage between Spanish men and Indian noblewomen was encouraged in colonial Spanish America. The descendants of such marriages make up the majority of the population of most Latin American countries.

How they make their women work

How they marry the Indians

How they confess them

How they apply penitence

They fight

They get drunk with half-castes

There are also some good Christians

The Franciscans are charitable

Above: the misconduct and cruelties of Spanish priests in Peru are irreverently depicted in a series of drawings made about the year 1613 by the Inca artist Guaman Poma. The last four drawings show that there were also good men among the clergy, especially the Franciscan mendicants who were "poor and beg like the rest of the poor."

was treated with royal honors. The viceroy was assisted by an *audiencia*—a civil court—and an advisory body. The smaller administrative divisions were headed by governors and mayors. All these officials, as well as the higher officials of the Church, were usually Spanish-born.

The Viceroy of New Spain held court in Mexico City. His authority reached from Texas to Costa Rica. The Viceroy of Peru, with his palace in Lima, controlled almost the whole of South America (with the exception of Venezuela and Portuguese Brazil).

In theory, as well as in practice, the authority of the King of Spain was supreme in the Americas. His wishes were transmitted to his American kingdoms by the Council of the Indies—a powerful body whose functions included the issuing of laws, the supervision of the Church, justice, and finance, and the direction of trade and shipping.

It was the end of an era. The swarm of officials that had plagued Cortes in New Spain now had access to South and Central America as well. But the new laws they introduced came too late to save the Indians. Manco Capac II, the Inca puppet ruler, who had so nearly succeeded in destroying the Spaniards at Cuzco in 1536,

They cruelly punish little children

They gamble

A good aged vicar of eighty years

A pious hermit begs for the poor

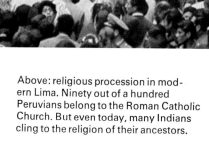

carried on a guerilla resistance until his death at the hands of Spanish forces nine years later. Thereafter, the few Indians who continued to resist were forced to retreat deeper and deeper into the Andes Mountains. Their last strongholds were in the mountains between the Urubamba and the Apurimac rivers. Machu Picchu was almost certainly one of them. The impenetrable nature of these mountains offered no incentive to Spaniards intent upon the rapid acquisition of wealth, and it was their failure to penetrate this area that gave rise to rumors of lost cities and hidden hoards of Inca gold. The majority of Indians, however, passively accepted the destruction of their civilization and the condition of virtual serfdom that followed.

The first Spaniards who came to the Americas were conquerors. They were men of a feudal age not yet ended, who stood on the threshold of an age of discovery. Individually they were adventurers who financed their own expeditions and staked everything on one throw. They knew with great exactness what they wanted. They wanted gold, and they sought it ruthlessly. In the cases of Mexico and Peru, they knew they could win only through desperate meas-

Above: religious procession in modern Lima. Ninety out of a hundred Peruvians belong to the Roman Catholic Church. But even today, many Indians cling to the religion of their ancestors.

159

ures. They were willing to risk their lives to achieve their ends. Something of the pain they caused they also endured.

The natural abilities of the conquistadors, as well as their luck, varied widely. Some of them were obvious incompetents. Others gave hints of genius. They ranged from the illiterate Pizarro (perhaps the boldest adventurer of them all), to the cultured and sophisticated Cortes. But none of them deviated from the broad pattern. All had those qualities that in the circumstances made for their short-term success—an overpowering lust for gold, a religious fanaticism, a hardness toward self and toward others, and a heroic discipline.

With the assassination of Pizarro in 1541, the age of the conquistador was drawing to its end. The period of discovery and conquest had been relatively short. Within 50 years a whole new world, vast in size and spanning two continents, had been opened up.

Above: in this view of the Spanish conquest, Diego Rivera, the modern Mexican artist, depicts Hernando Cortes as a malformed and grotesque figure. In the burst of national feeling that swept Mexico during the 1800's and 1900's, the role of the Spanish conquistador was denigrated.

The Explorers

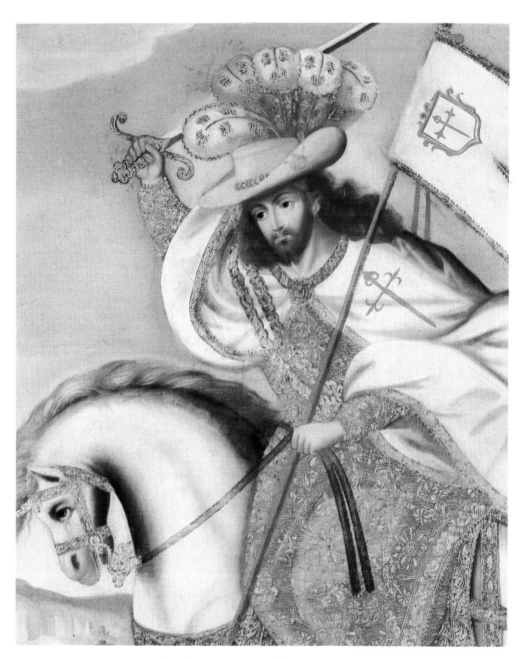

Santiago, patron saint of the conquistadors.

ALARCÓN, HERNANDO DE

1500–(?)   Spain

1540: Sailed up the coast of western Mexico, carrying supplies for Coronado's land expedition. While exploring the Gulf of California, confirmed that Lower California was a peninsula and not an island as had been previously believed. Navigated the Colorado's lower course to the north of the Gila River. Returned to New Spain without making contact with Coronado's forces.
See map on pages 88–89

ALMAGRO, DIEGO DE

1475–1538   Spain

1524–1525: Was a partner with Francisco Pizarro on his first attempt to reach the Inca empire. Explored the Pacific coast of Colombia. Returned to Panama without reaching Peru.
1526–1527: Took part in second voyage to Peru. After two return trips to Panama to replenish troops and supplies, Almagro rejoined Pizarro at the island of Gallo. They reached the Inca city of Tumbes, and sailed farther south to present-day Santa.
1531–1533: Took part in the conquest of Peru, joining Pizarro's expedition at Cajamarca. With Pizarro, marched on the Inca capital at Cuzco.
1535–1537: Conquered Chile. Led expedition south from Cuzco along the shores of Lake Titicaca into present-day Bolivia and Argentina. Continued south as far as present-day Santiago. Sent small party to the south before returning to Peru along the coast. Became the first white man to cross the barren Atacama Desert.
See map on page 122

ALVARADO, PEDRO DE

1485(?)–1541   Spain

1519–1521: Joined Cortes in his conquest of Mexico. Was left in command of Mexico City while Cortes defeated Velásquez' forces at Veracruz.
1523–1527: Led expedition south into Guatemala, where he defeated the Maya Indians. Appointed governor of Guatemala.
See maps on pages 76–77, 122

ANDAGOYA, PASCUAL DE

1495–1548   Spain

1522: Commanded the first official government survey south of Panama. He reached a point south of the Gulf of San Miguel and met Indians who told him of the rich Inca empire. Reached as far as the Biru River in present-day Colombia. Biru may be the original form of Peru.
See map on page 122

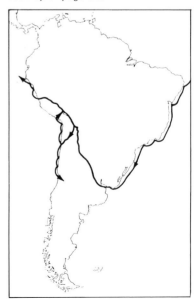

BINGHAM, HIRAM

1875–1956   United States
1906–1924: Made six expeditions to
South America.
1911: Discovered the "lost city" of
the Inca, Machu Picchu, high in the
Peruvian Andes.
See map bottom of previous page

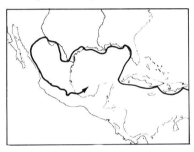

CABEZA DE VACA, ÁLVAR NÚÑEZ

1490(?)–1557(?)   Spain
1528–1536: Was a member of an
expedition that attempted to explore
Florida. Was shipwrecked on an island
off the Texas coast, and captured by the
Indians. Finally, with three companions,
made his way back to Mexico on foot.
Reported that gold and iron were to be
found north of Mexico.

CÁRDENAS, GARCÍA LÓPEZ DE

dates unknown   Spain
1540–1542: Accompanied Coronado
on his expedition into the present-day
Southwest United States. Explored
Hopi territories of northern Arizona.
Was the first white man to penetrate
the Grand Canyon.
See map on pages 88–89

COLUMBUS, CHRISTOPHER

1451–1506   Genoa
1492–1493: Sailed west in the service
of Spain in search of the Indies.
Discovered San Salvador, Cuba, and
Hispaniola although, to the end of his
life, he believed he had reached
the Orient.
1493–1496: On his second voyage west
discovered Dominica, Guadeloupe,
and Mariagalante, and sighted the
Virgin Islands. Set up a colony on
Hispaniola.
1498–1500: On his third voyage across

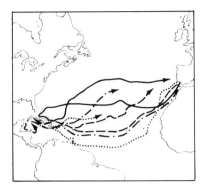

the Atlantic, discovered Trinidad and
sighted the coast of South America
(which he thought part of a great
continent). Traveled on to Hispaniola.
1500: Was arrested and divested of his
position as Viceroy of the Indies.
1502–1504: Final voyage west.
Forbidden to revisit Hispaniola, he
traveled down the coast of Central
America.

CÓRDOBA, FRANCISCO HERNÁNDEZ DE

(?)–1517   Spain
1517: Appointed by a group of fortune
hunters to command an expedition to
the west of Cuba. Discovered and
sailed up the coast of Yucatán.
He was the first Spaniard to
encounter traces of the Maya
civilization.
See maps on pages 76–77, 88–89

CORONADO, FRANCISCO VÁSQUEZ DE

1510–1554   Spain
1538: Was appointed governor of New
Galicia, a northwest province of New
Spain.
1540–1542: Led an expedition into
the American Southwest in search of
the legendary Seven Cities of Cibola.
Traveled through what is today Arizona
and New Mexico before reaching the
Zuñi Pueblo. The following spring, he
led his forces across the Great Plains
into what is now Kansas, in a futile
search for the rich kingdom of
Quivira. Some of his men discovered
the Grand Canyon.

CORTES, HERNANDO

1485–1547   Spain
1504: Went to Santo Domingo on the
island of Hispaniola in the West Indies.
1511: Took part in conquest of Cuba.
1519–1520: Commissioned by
Velásquez to lead an expedition to
conquer Mexico. Sailed from Cuba to
Cozumel Island off the coast of Yucatán.
Then followed the coast to the island of
San Juan de Ulua. He founded the city
of Veracruz, the first colony in New
Spain. Marched inland, through
Tlaxacala where he made allies of the
local Indians. Crossing the Sierra Madre
Mountains he reached the Aztec capital
of Tenochtitlán, captured the emperor
Montezuma, and established Spanish
control. While Cortes was in Veracruz,
the Aztec rose up against the Spaniards.
Cortes returned but was unable to
quell the rebellion and he and his men
were forced to flee the capital.
1521: Laid siege to Tenochtitlán and
destroyed the city. Founded the capital
of New Spain, Mexico City, on its ruins.
1524–1526: Led an expedition into
Honduras, traveling 1,300 miles across
difficult terrain.
1535: Commanded an expedition that
founded the first Spanish colony in
Lower California.
See maps on pages 76–77, 78, 88–89

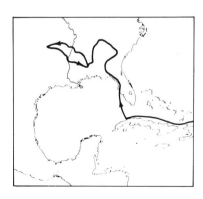

DE SOTO, HERNANDO

1499–1542   Spain
1531–1533: Served under Pizarro
during the conquest of Peru.
1539–1542: Led an expedition to
Florida. Explored the Southeast United

States, becoming the first white man to cross the Mississippi River.

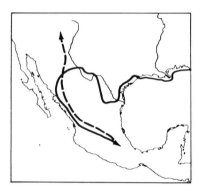

ESTEVANICO
(?)–1539   Morocco
1528–1536: Accompanied Narváez and Cabeza on an expedition in Florida. With Cabeza crossed half of the American continent on foot after being shipwrecked off the Texas coast.
1539: With Fray Marcos de Niza, led a party into the Southwest United States in search of the Seven Cities of Cibola. Reached a Zuñi Pueblo near present-day Gallup, New Mexico which was thought to be the fabled city. Was murdered by the Zuñi Indians.

GRIJALVA, JUAN DE
1489(?)–1527   Spain
1518: Commissioned by Velásquez to explore the coast of Mexico following Córdoba's discovery of Yucatán. Sailed along east coast from Yucatán to what is now Cape Roxo. Learned of the Aztec empire located in the interior and met with emissaries of Montezuma. First to give the region the name *New Spain*.
See maps on pages 76–77, 88–89

JIMÉNEZ DE QUESADA, GONZALO
1499–1579   Spain
1536–1538: Set out to explore the upper reaches of the Magdalena River, Colombia's chief river. Reached the high plains of the central Colombian Andes—the home of the Chibcha Indians. Conquered the Chibcha in 1538 and founded Bogotá, the capital

of modern Bolivia.
See map on page 122

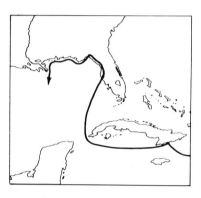

NARVÁEZ, PÁNFILO DE
1470–1528   Spain
1511: With Velásquez, helped to conquer Cuba.
1528: Led an unsuccessful expedition to explore Florida. Marched inland and was cut off from his ships. Built five crude boats and sailed along the coast to what is now Texas. Was drowned in the Gulf of Mexico, but some of his men reached New Spain.

NIZA, FRAY MARCOS DE
(?)–1558   Italy
1539: With Estevanico and a small party of Pima Indians explored what is today the Southwest United States in search of the Seven Cities of Cibola. Proceeded up the western coast of Mexico, crossed the Yaqui River and followed the Sonora River. Crossed

present-day Arizona and ascended the Colorado Plateau into New Mexico. Reached the Zuñi Pueblo near present-day Gallup, New Mexico. Returned to New Spain claiming to have found a city of vast wealth.
1540: Led Coronado and a large conquering force to the Zuñi Pueblo he had discovered the previous year.

OLID, CRISTÓBAL DE
1488–1524   Spain
1519–1521: Served under Cortes during the conquest of Mexico.
1524: Sent by Cortes to explore the Yucatán and found a colony in Honduras. Penetrated into Honduras where he subdued the Maya and declared himself independent of Cortes. Was executed in 1524.
See map on pages 76–77

ORELLANA, FRANCISCO DE
1500(?)–1546   Spain
1541–1542: Accompanied Gonzalo Pizarro on his expedition in search of the kingdom of El Dorado. Continued journey by boat down the Napo and Coca rivers to the valley of the Amazon. Explored the course of the Amazon from the Andes to the Atlantic Ocean, becoming the first white man to accomplish this feat.
See map on page 122

PIZARRO, FRANCISCO
1478(?)–1541   Spain
1502: Arrived at the island of Hispaniola.
1524–1525: Set out on his first attempt to reach Peru. Sailed as far as Colombia, exploring the coast along the way.
1526–1528: With Bartolome Ruiz as captain, sailed southwest from Panama landing at a more favorable spot on the Colombian coast. Led a plundering expedition inland, while Almagro returned to Panama and Ruiz sailed farther south. Spent some time on the island of Gallo off the coast of Colombia awaiting reinforcements. Defying the governor of Panama's order to return, he and Almagro continued south to the Inca city of Tumbes in present-day Peru before

returning to Panama. Sailed to Spain
to obtain royal permission to explore
and conquer Peru.
1531–1533: Sailed from Panama to
conquer Peru. Began his campaign
from the city of Tumbes. Founded the
city of San Miguel before advancing to
Cajamarca, where he captured and
executed Atahualpa, the reigning Inca.
1533: With reinforcements brought
by Almagro, marched from Cajamarca
to the Inca capital of Cuzco high
in the Andes.
1535: Founded the city of Lima on the
banks of the Rimac River.
See map on page 122

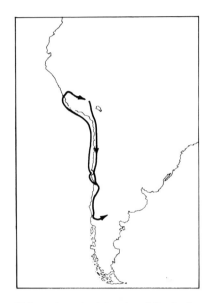

PIZARRO, GONZALO
1506(?)–1548   Spain
1531–1533: Accompanied his brother
during the conquest of the Inca empire.
1541–1542: Was appointed governor
of Quito, in present-day Ecuador. Led an
expedition into northwestern South
America in search of the kingdom of
El Dorado. Set out from Quito, crossed
the eastern Cordillera of the Andes and
descended into the Amazon basin.
Reached the banks of the Coca River
and followed it to its juncture with the
Napo. Abandoned by Orellana, he and
his men were forced to fight their way
back to Quito on foot with few supplies
and weapons.
See map on page 122

RUIZ, BARTOLOME
dates unknown   Spain
1526–1527: Piloted the ship that carried
Pizarro to the coast of Colombia.
Sailed southwest to avoid the coastal
currents. Continued farther south to a
point just beyond the equator where he
encountered an Inca balsa raft far out
to sea thus becoming the first Spaniard
to make contact with the Inca.
1531–1533: Accompanied Pizarro on
his conquest of Peru.
See map on page 122

VALDIVIA, PEDRO DE
1500(?)–1553   Spain
1540: Commissioned by Francisco
Pizarro to found a colony in Chile.
Led his men south along the Pacific
coast. Crossed the Atacama Desert in

Chile and reached the city of Copiapó.
1541: Continued farther south to
central Chile where he founded the
city of Santiago. Established the port of
Valparaíso, 60 miles from Santiago.
1545: Established the city of La Serena
in the Coquimbo Valley.
1550: Explored southern Chile and
founded the city of Concepción.
See map on page 122

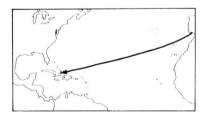

VELÁSQUEZ, DIEGO
1465(?)–1524   Spain
1493: Sailed to Hispaniola with
Columbus on his second voyage to the
New World.
1511: Led an expedition to conquer
the island of Cuba.
1511–1521, 1523–1524: As governor
of Cuba sent out expeditions under
Córdoba, Grijalva, and Cortes.

Glossary

adelantado: A provincial governor appointed by the Spanish king. It was a position of considerable power and importance in the colonies.

adobe: Spanish name for red bricks dried in the sun, or for a house built with such bricks. Adobe was a characteristic of ancient American architecture, in Peru as well as in North America.

alpaca: Smaller, slimmer version of the llama. The alpaca has been domesticated since the time of the Inca. Its soft, silky wool, together with that of the related wild vicuña, was reserved by the Inca for the use of royalty and nobility.

altiplano: A region of high, windswept plateaus between the western and eastern Cordilleras of the Andes Mountains. The altiplano lies mainly in western Bolivia but extends north into Peru and south into Argentina. The climate is cold and inhospitable and little vegetation grows. Location of Lake Titicaca, South America's largest inland lake.

Amazons: In Greek mythology, a race of female warriors who fought with the ancient Greeks and made slaves of the men they conquered. A similar Indian myth tells of a tribe of female warriors in South America. Orellana's claims to have seen the Amazons on his trip down the Amazon River may have been inspired by his encounter with the long-haired beardless male warriors of the river tribes.

Araucanian Indians: A large group of Indians who lived in Chile and Argentina at the time of the Spanish conquest. They are famous for their long and successful resistance to Spanish domination. They were not subdued until the late 1800's.

Arawak Indians: First American Indians encountered by the Europeans. The Arawak lived on the islands of the Caribbean Sea and in the Amazon River Valley. Many Arawak died from disease, privation, and forced labor after the Spanish invasion.

audiencia: A court of judges appointed by the Spanish king. It was the highest tribunal in New Spain, and was composed of a president and four associate judges. The audiencia was first established in Mexico in 1527.

balsa raft: A raft of light wood lashed together that was used by the Inca along the Peruvian coast and on Lake Titicaca.

brigantine: A small, partially decked sailing vessel, propelled by oars and sails. Cortes built brigantines and used them in his conquest of Mexico. These had a small gun mounted forward and carried a crew of 23.

buffalo: Common name for the bison, a large wild animal with a massive head and neck and humped shoulders. Great herds of buffalo once roamed the North American continent. Coronado and his men encountered these herds while searching for the Seven Cities of Cibola.

cacao: An evergreen tree whose seeds or beans are used to make chocolate or cocoa. Cacao trees are cultivated in Central and South America. Before the Spanish conquest, cacao beans were used as money in Mexico and Central America.

cacique: An Indian chieftain.

Ce Acatl: "One Reed." According to Aztec legend, the year in which the god Quetzalcoatl would return to Mexico. Cortes landed in Mexico in 1519, a Ce Acatl year.

Chibcha Indians: Lived on the high plains of the central Colombian Andes. The Chibcha worked gold, drilled emeralds, made pottery and baskets, and wove textiles. They were conquered by the Spaniards under Jiménez de Quesada in 1538.

Chimu civilization: A powerful Indian state on the northern Peruvian coast. The Chimu civilization was at least as old as the Inca's. It was conquered by the Inca under Tupac Inca.

chinampas: Small, man-made islands of rich, moist earth constructed by the Aztec in the city of Tenochtitlán. These "floating gardens" gradually became attached to the shallow lake bottom, thus extending the area of the Aztec capital.

city-state: An autonomous state made up of a city and the surrounding area. The city-state was the political unit of the Maya. The Aztec empire was a loose confederation of city-states.

codex: A manuscript book. In Mexico, a codex is an Indian painted book or an ancient historical source that is based on an Indian manuscript. Codices were used to record Mexican history, the genealogy and descendants of kings and royal personages, and Indian laws, rites, and ceremonies. They were pictorial and were essentially only lists of events that served as memory aids to Indian historians.

conquistadors: Spanish explorers who conquered various regions of Latin America during the 1500's. *Conquistador* is a Spanish word meaning "conqueror."

Cordillera: A group of mountain ranges, usually the principal mountain group of a continent. From the Spanish word *cuerda* meaning "cord" or "chain." Once used in America to mean only the Andes Mountains, but now generally applied. The mountain ranges of the Andes are still called *Cordilleras*.

corregidor: Governor of a city or province, appointed by the Spanish king or his representatives.

Council of the Indies: A powerful legislative body appointed by the Spanish king to control the colonies in the New World. The Council issued laws, supervised the Church, administered justice, controlled finance, and directed trade and shipping.

coya: The queen of the Inca, sister-bride of the emperor. The heir to the Inca throne had to be an offspring of the union between the emperor and his coya or official wife.

El Dorado: City or country of fabulous riches believed by early explorers to exist somewhere in South America. Supposed to be ruled by a king, also named El Dorado, the gilded one, because he was said to annoint himself with gold dust. Today, the name is used to designate a place of fabulous wealth.

encomienda: A social and economic system based on European feudalism and established throughout Spanish America. It gave Spaniards grants of land and Indian laborers. These were theoretically free but were required to give the Spaniards service and tribute. Many Indians suffered greatly under the system.

flowery wars: A form of ceremonial warfare practiced by the Aztec and certain enemy states. Their only object was that of capturing warriors to use as sacrificial victims on the altars of Mexico or in the winning state. Soldiers did their best to take the enemy alive for this purpose.

friars: Spanish priests of the Roman Catholic religion who accompanied the conquistadors to the New World in order to convert the Indians to Christianity.

guanaco: Wild South American member of the camel family from which the llama and alpaca are believed to derive. Fawn-colored and about four feet high, they are adept at climbing and swimming. They were once hunted in vast numbers by the Inca, and later by the Spaniards.

hieroglyphics: A system of writing mainly in pictorial characters.

Hopi Indians: Pueblo Indians of the American southwest, first encountered by Tovar and his men during their search for treasure.

Huitzilopochtli: The favorite Aztec deity, was god of war and of the sun. He required the sacrifice of human blood and hearts in order that the sun would rise each morning.

Indians: Name given by Christopher Columbus to the inhabitants of the New World because he believed he had reached India.

llama: A member of the camel family that lives in South America. The llama was domesticated by the Indians hundreds of years ago. It is most useful as a pack animal because it is capable of carrying about 100 pounds and is sure-footed on the mountain trails.

Mixtec: One of the most ancient and highly developed civilizations of Mexico, the Mixtec "People of the Clouds" lived in the highlands of what is today the state of Oaxaca. They produced fabulous gold work and were the authors of seven of the 16 codices that have survived to the present time.

Nahuatl: The language of the Aztec people. From it came such English words as tomato, chocolate, and chili.

Pima Indians: Live along the Gila and Salt rivers near Phoenix, Arizona. The Pima developed an advanced way of life around A.D. 1000. They built substantial villages of adobe pit houses and farmed with the aid of a system of irrigation canals.

Plains Indians: General name given to the Indians who lived between the Mississippi River and the Rocky Mountains. Many of the Plains Indians were nomads who followed the migration of the great buffalo herds.

pre-Columbian America: Name given to designate the history of the New World before its discovery by Christopher Columbus.

Pueblo Indians: *Pueblo* is the Spanish word for "village," and was the name given by early Spanish explorers to the Indian settlements they discovered in the Southwest United States. The name was extended to include the inhabitants of these settlements. The Pueblo Indians encountered by Coronado and his men were a settled people who had developed a complex way of life. They are famous for their many-storied buildings—the prototype of the modern apartment house.

Quechuan: The official language of the Inca empire. Leaders of each tribe conquered by the Inca were required to learn the Quechuan language.

Quetzalcoatl: "The Plumed Serpent," was the Aztec god of learning and of the priesthood. According to legend Quetzalcoatl had sailed across the sea but had promised to return. Montezuma believed Cortes to be the returned god.

quipu: A device used by the Inca for keeping accounts. It consisted of one main strand of rope from which others were hung. Knots were tied in the string to indicate the number of a given item. The quipu was used also in the recording of Inca history, the preservation of tradition, and the relaying of messages.

Quivira: A legendary city of gold said to be located somewhere in the American Midwest. Coronado and his men marched for Quivira in 1541.

regidors: Members of powerful town or city councils set up by the Spaniards throughout the New World.

repartimiento: An allotment of land and Indians granted to the conquistadors in return for service to the king of Spain.

requerimento: A document issued by the Spanish monarch that invited the Indians to become Christians and subjects of Spain. If they refused, the document ordered the conquistadors to make war upon them.

Seven Cities of Cibola: Legendary cities of great wealth that were believed to exist somewhere to the north of Mexico, in what is now the Southwest United States. In 1540, Francisco Vásquez de Coronado set out in search of these cities and in the course of his travels explored large sections of Arizona and New Mexico.

tambos: Rest stations with storehouses and shelters situated at regular intervals along the Inca's vast network of highways.

teules: Nahuatl word for gods. The Spanish conquistadors were believed to be teules by the Indians of Mexico.

Tejas Indians: The Indian word *tejas* means friends or "allies." The Tejas formed a group of united Indian tribes that lived in what is now the northeastern part of Texas. The state of Texas received its name from the Spanish pronunciation of *tejas*.

Tiahuanaco civilization: An ancient Indian civilization that existed along the shores of Lake Titicaca in Bolivia from the A.D. 300's to the 900's. It had large stone buildings, decorated with carvings of animals and geometric figures. It declined rapidly after the 900's. Inca architecture was influenced by the ruins of Tiahuanacan buildings.

viceroy: An official who rules a province or colony in the name of the monarch.

vicuña: Small, orange-red colored relative of the guanaco, highly valued for its fine silky wool. Found in Peru, Ecuador, and Bolivia.

Index

Picture Credits

Listed below are the sources of all the illustrations in this book. To identify the source of a particular illustration, first find the relevant page on the diagram opposite. The number in black in the appropriate position on that page refers to the credit as listed below.

1 Aldus Archives
2 Courtesy of The American Museum of Natural History
3 Ferdinand Anton, München
4 Archives de la Indias, Sevilla
5 Barnaby's Picture Library
6 The Bettmann Archive
7 Biblioteca Medicea Laurenxiana, Firenze
8 Biblioteca Nacional, Madrid/Photo Mas
9 Biblioteca Nazionale Centrale, Firenze
10 Bibliothèque Nationale, Paris
11 Bodleian Library, Oxford
12 Reproduced by courtesy of the Trustees of the British Museum
13 British Museum/Photo R. B. Fleming © Aldus Books
14 British Museum/Photo John Freeman © Aldus Books
15 British Museum/Michael Holford Library
16 Harvey Caplin, Alameda, New Mexico
17 La Catedral, Lima/Photo Peter Larsen, F.R.P.S., F.R.G.S.
18 The William L. Clements Library, University of Michigan
19 Courtesy Celso Pastor de la Torre
20 Dienst Voor 's Rijks Verspreide Kunstvoorwerpen, Den Haag
21 Werner Forman
22 Geographical Projects Limited, London
23 From *Mexican Art*, The Hamlyn Group/Photo Constantino Reyes-Valerio
24 National Museum of Anthropology, Mexico City. From *Mexican Art*, The Hamlyn Group/Photo Constantino Reyes-Valerio
25 The John Hillelson Agency
26 Collection of the Duke of Infantado/Photo Mas
27 The John Judkyn Memorial,

Freshford Manor, Bath/Photo Mike Busselle © Aldus Books
28 Keystone
29 Peter Larsen, F.R.O.S , F.R.G.S.
30 Collection Mujica Gallo, Peru/ Michael Holford Library
31 Museo de America, Madrid/Photo Mas
32 Museo Histórico Regional del Cuzco, Calle Heladeros, Peru
33 Museum für Völkerkunde, Vienna
34 National History Museum, Mexico
35 Nuestra Senora de Copacabana, Lima/Photo José Casals
36 Orion Press Inc., New York
37 Bild-Archiv der Österreichischen Nationalbibliothek, Wien
38 Peabody Museum, Harvard University
39 Picturepoint, London
40 From the Collection of the Roswell Museum and Art Center, Roswell, New Mexico
41 The Royal Geographical Society/ Photo Mike Busselle © Aldus Books
42 The Royal Library, Copenhagen
43 Courtesy The Royal Library, Copenhagen, Old Royal Collection 2232 (Poma de Ayala) and Victor von Hagen, *Ancient Sun Kingdom of the Americas*, Thames and Hudson Ltd., London, 1962
44 Property of Willmar Sick, Baltimore
45 The property of Miss M. L. A. Strickland, by courtesy of whom is reproduced and is on loan to the Ministry of Public Building and Works, hung in the British Embassy, Mexico/Photo Copytek © Aldus Books
46 Universitetsbiblioteket, Uppsala
47 Business Men's Assurance Company, Kansas City/Artist: Byron B. Wolfe, Leawood, Kansas by courtesy of the artist

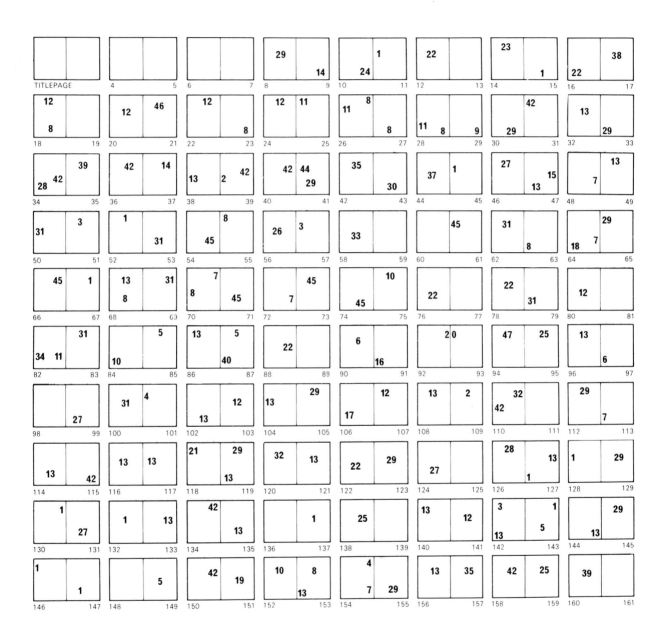